ASSERTIVENESS *for*
EARTH ANGELS

ALSO BY DOREEN VIRTUE

Books/Calendar/Kits/Oracle Board

Living Pain Free
(with Robert Reeves, N.D.; available March 2015)

The Lightworker's Survival Guide
(with Charles Virtue; available January 2015)

Angels of Abundance
(with Grant Virtue; available August 2014)

The Big Book of Angel Tarot
(with Radleigh Valentine; available July 2014)

Angel Dreams (with Melissa Virtue; available April 2014)

Angel Astrology 101
(with Yasmin Boland; available March 2014)

Angels of Love (with Grant Virtue available January 2014)

Angel Detox (with Robert Reeves, N.D.; available January 2014)

How to Heal a Grieving Heart (with James Van Praagh)

The Essential Doreen Virtue Collection

Whispers from Above 2014 Calendar

The Miracles of Archangel Gabriel

Mermaids 101

Flower Therapy (with Robert Reeves, N.D.)

Mary, Queen of Angels

Saved by an Angel

The Angel Therapy® Handbook

Angel Words (with Grant Virtue)

Archangels 101

The Healing Miracles of Archangel Raphael

The Art of Raw Living Food (with Jenny Ross)

Signs from Above (with Charles Virtue)

The Miracles of Archangel Michael

Angel Numbers 101

Solomon's Angels (a novel)

My Guardian Angel (with Amy Oscar)

Audio/CD Programs

The Healing Miracles of Archangel Raphael
Angel Therapy® Meditations
Archangels 101 (abridged audio book)
Fairies 101 (abridged audio book)
Goddesses & Angels (abridged audio book)
Angel Medicine (available as both 1- and 2-CD sets)
Angels among Us (with Michael Toms)
Messages from Your Angels (abridged audio book)
Past-Life Regression with the Angels
Divine Prescriptions
The Romance Angels
Connecting with Your Angels
Manifesting with the Angels
Karma Releasing
Healing Your Appetite, Healing Your Life
Healing with the Angels
Divine Guidance
Chakra Clearing

DVD Program

How to Give an Angel Card Reading

Oracle Cards (divination cards and guidebook)

Earth Angels Tarot Cards
(with Radleigh Valentine; available December 2014)
Past Life Oracle Cards (with Brian Weiss, M.D.;
available October 2014)
Cherub Angel Cards for Children (available June 2014)
Angels of Abundance Tarot Cards
(with Radleigh Valentine; available May 2014)
Talking to Heaven Mediumship Cards (with James Van Praagh)
Archangel Power Tarot Cards (with Radleigh Valentine)

Flower Therapy Oracle Cards (with Robert Reeves, N.D.)
Indigo Angel Oracle Cards (with Charles Virtue)
Angel Dreams Oracle Cards (with Melissa Virtue)
Mary, Queen of Angels Oracle Cards
Angel Tarot Cards
(with Radleigh Valentine and Steve A. Roberts)
The Romance Angels Oracle Cards
Life Purpose Oracle Cards
Archangel Raphael Healing Oracle Cards
Archangel Michael Oracle Cards
Angel Therapy® Oracle Cards
Magical Messages from the Fairies Oracle Cards
Ascended Masters Oracle Cards
Daily Guidance from Your Angels Oracle Cards
Saints & Angels Oracle Cards
Magical Unicorns Oracle Cards
Goddess Guidance Oracle Cards
Archangel Oracle Cards
Magical Mermaids and Dolphins Oracle Cards
Messages from Your Angels Oracle Cards
Healing with the Fairies Oracle Cards
Healing with the Angels Oracle Cards

All of the above are available at your local bookstore,
or may be ordered by visiting:

Hay House USA: **www.hayhouse.com®**
Hay House Australia: **www.hayhouse.com.au**
Hay House UK: **www.hayhouse.co.uk**
Hay House South Africa: **www.hayhouse.co.za**
Hay House India: **www.hayhouse.co.in**

Doreen's website: **www.AngelTherapy.com**

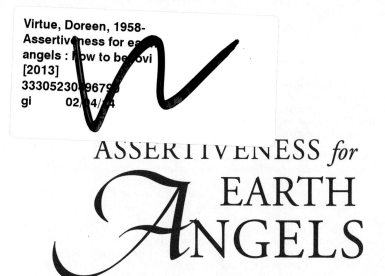

ASSERTIVENESS *for* EARTH ANGELS

HOW TO BE LOVING INSTEAD OF "TOO NICE"

DOREEN VIRTUE

HAY HOUSE, INC.
Carlsbad, California • New York City
London • Sydney • Johannesburg
Vancouver • Hong Kong • New Delhi

Published and distributed in the United States by: Hay House, Inc.:
www.hayhouse.com® • **Published and distributed in Australia by:**
Hay House Australia Pty. Ltd.: www.hayhouse.com.au • **Published
and distributed in the United Kingdom by:** Hay House UK, Ltd.:
www.hayhouse.co.uk • **Published and distributed in the Republic
of South Africa by:** Hay House SA (Pty), Ltd.: www.hayhouse.co.za
• **Distributed in Canada by:** Raincoast: www.raincoast.com • **Published in India by:** Hay House Publishers India: www.hayhouse.co.in

Cover design: Tricia Breidenthal • Interior design: Riann Bender
Cover artwork: Howard David Johnson

Library of Congress Cataloging-in-Publication Data

Virtue, Doreen.
  Assertiveness for earth angels : how to be loving instead of "too
nice" / Doreen Virtue. -- 1st edition.
    pages cm
  ISBN 978-1-4019-2880-3 (hardcover : alk. paper) 1. Success.
2. Assertiveness (Psychology) I. Title.
  BJ1611.2.V57 2013
  158.2--dc23
                            2013022689

Hardcover ISBN: 978-1-4019-2880-3

16 15 14 13   5 4 3 2
1st edition, November 2013
2nd edition, November 2013

Printed in the United States of America

To the power of God, which
resides within you and everyone.

CONTENTS

PART III: Being Assertive Out in the World

PART IV: Life Tools and Guidance for Earth Angels

$\mathcal{P}$REFACE

Earth Angels and Conflict Phobia

I was at a dinner party with several famous spiritual authors. Across from me was a well-known television psychic, and sitting next to her was Esther Hicks (of Abraham-Hicks fame). I was uncomfortable because the psychic had publicly disparaged my work in the past, but I sat there anyway, pretending that everything was okay and trying to make pleasant conversation with her. But she didn't play nice with me, and everything she said to me felt like a put-down. Finally, the psychic looked right at me and announced loudly to the table, "I just hate people who love unicorns and rainbows!"

Awkward silence. My energy fell. My face grew hot.

Then Esther Hicks saved the day. She looked directly at the psychic and said with perfect strength: "Well, maybe that's because you haven't yet had the experience of unicorns and rainbows!" There wasn't an ounce of sarcasm or placating in Esther's voice or energy. She was speaking purely from a place of fearless and centered power.

Everyone at the table was quiet. I wanted to run away or duck under the table.

Then the psychic shifted her body weight, sighed, and replied, "Hmm, perhaps you're right."

I looked at Esther with gratitude for teaching me one of my most important life lessons that evening. She showed me how to maintain dignity and inner peace in the face of harsh energy. Since then, I've devoted myself to studying and practicing this spiritual art. In this book, I'll share with you everything I've learned.

I discovered that there's a vast difference between being "nice" and being "loving." I had lived my life as a "nice girl," covering up my feelings to protect others, and sugarcoating what I said to avoid conflict. "If you can't say anything nice, don't say anything at all" was my philosophy. I respected authority without question, and stuffed down my feelings. Then those pent-up feelings would become unbearable and I'd either confront the person who triggered them or leave the relationship.

I thought I was being nice.

I wasn't.

I was being fearful, which is the opposite of love.

As I prayed for help with my relationships, I began to receive important life lessons. I'd hear them as intuitive "downloads," meaning that a knowingness or *Aha!* insight would suddenly appear. Sometimes the lessons would be accompanied by visual or auditory teachings. I'd see visions or hear a voice in my right ear, which is the way the angels have communicated with me since I was a child.

The first lesson I learned was that sensitive people like you and me were "sent" here as Earth Angels with an important mission: to defuse and reduce conflict on this planet. Our mission doesn't involve ignoring conflict. It involves *resolving* it.

We Earth Angels are like loving-but-firm parents sent here to express God's benevolent power to help others. Here's an example by way of analogy: If a child wants to only eat candy and says that doing so makes him happy, would a good parent allow this?

Of course not. Even if the child cries or gets angry, a good parent must say no to the request to continually eat candy. The parent may moderate this response by occasionally allowing candy, or may substitute healthier treats. However the situation is handled, though, it comes down to the parent being strong enough to say no.

That metaphor is applicable to our life mission. When there's conflict on the planet—whether it's an argument between partners or feuds between countries—it's akin to little children throwing tantrums because they're not getting their way. We as Earth Angels need to assume the parental role, bringing about a peaceful resolution.

Managing conflict can be uncomfortable because Earth Angels are so attuned to energy. We can feel when others are stressed, angry, sad, or uncomfortable. Their emotional energy affects us directly. Fortunately, we can use our awareness to shift this discomfort in a healthier and more peaceful direction.

Remember the metaphor of the caring parent: she gets involved in her child's conflict because she loves him. With a loving heart, you step in and tell the truth—whether it's with your child, a friend, your spouse, or a co-worker. You reveal your real feelings, because you know it's the only route to a long-lasting and healthy relationship.

Holding your feelings in is like putting a steadily increasing amount of air into a balloon. There's a limit to how much air the balloon will hold before it explodes!

Making Peace with Conflict

Adversity pushes us to become stronger, and I've had my share of adverse experiences! I've been tricked, manipulated, sued, gossiped about, betrayed, lied to, abandoned, stalked, used, abused, and subjected to just about every other painful situation you can think of. Yet, instead of being bitter, I've grown stronger and wiser with each experience.

In fact, I've learned that when your back is pushed up against the wall (metaphorically), you find your inner strength. A couple of years after Esther Hicks defended me, I was going through a divorce in which my ex-husband's lawyer was viciously going after every penny I'd ever earned . . . and *would* ever earn. They were demanding my home, my entire retirement savings, and half my future earnings for life.

My conflict-phobic self normally allowed angry people to take whatever they wanted from me, in exchange for peace. *But this time I had no choice but to stand up for myself.* I had to face the conflict head-on. I prayed constantly for help, and I clearly heard Archangel Michael say that he was watching over me.

The situation was frightening and enraging. I endured process servers, depositions, and courtrooms. I felt emotions that I'd never previously experienced. I remembered past lifetimes of persecution.

At first, I was angry with him for "doing this to me." I felt like a complete victim.

I finally awoke from my Earth Angel "bubble" and realized that these negative things were happening in my life because I wasn't listening to heaven. I realized that God and the angels had tried to forewarn me of every one of those painful experiences, and if I'd noticed their red-flag warnings, I would have avoided a lot of pain. So I had to do major forgiveness work to come to peace with myself for ultimately betraying my own self.

Once I forgave myself for getting in the situation that I was in, I found my inner power and strength. I stood up for myself and took charge of the situation! It wasn't about the outcome of the divorce. It was all about me learning how to face adversity with grace, poise, and peace.

Now I want to pass along this exciting information to you! You, too, can learn how to peacefully and lovingly take care of yourself in harsh circumstances.

I've learned so much from each painful occurrence, and this book is my opportunity to share this hard-earned knowledge with you. So my knowledge comes from firsthand experience, as well as working with people around the world.

I've interviewed, counseled, and taught thousands of Earth Angels across the globe. I've learned about the fears that drive us to act in self-sabotaging ways. And more important, I've learned how to *overcome* those fears and behaviors!

In my undergraduate psychology classes, I learned about and studied assertiveness in intellectual ways. I knew that assertiveness was a way to communicate my feelings and needs while respecting the rights of others. What took me years to learn was how to respect my own rights.

Are You an Earth Angel?

Earth Angel is a term I use to describe people who:

- Are highly sensitive

- Have an innocence in their outlook on love and life, which others may call naïve

- Believe in God's loving power (but aren't necessarily religious)

- Are gentle and caring

- See the best in others, including their hidden potentials

- Are trusting and optimistic

- Have been taken advantage of by those who use the Earth Angels' niceness for their own gain

- Have had painful relationship experiences, but still believe in true love and friendship

- Cherish the magical parts of spirituality, such as manifestation, unicorns, fairies, mermaids, and the like

- Feel called on a mission, with a sense of duty and stewardship toward others, including strangers
- Want everyone to be happy
- Are unhappy when others are upset
- Believe in fairness

Does that sound like you or someone you love?

-◈—◈-

Everyone is God's creation, and everyone has a purpose in life. Earth Angels are those who feel "sent" to Earth to bring about peace and create lasting positive change. Earth Angels use prayer, kindness, and love to help others. They can be any gender, sexual orientation, race, or religion. The common denominator is that Earth Angels feel compelled to help people and "make" them feel happy. In fact, *they* only feel happy when others are happy.

Sometimes Earth Angels are called *lightworkers*, which is a related term for highly sensitive people on a spiritual mission to bring peace to the world. To me, Earth Angels are a subcategory of lightworkers. They are the sweet, caring, and giving lightworkers of the world.

In my books *Earth Angels* and *Realms of the Earth Angels*, I describe the various realm origins of lightworkers, including that of the *incarnated angel*. In this book, the term *Earth Angel* encompasses all the realms. It also includes rainbow, crystal, and indigo children and adults.

In the ultimate sense, Earth Angels are performing an important mission collectively by walking around smiling and uplifting everyone with whom they come into contact. They are natural healers whose very presence heals people, animals, and plants. Earth Angels are highly connected with the Divine, and they're naturally intuitive. In fact, they're *so* connected that they're frequently ungrounded, spacey, and forgetful.

If you're an Earth Angel, you're obsessed with other people's happiness. If anyone you love is *un*happy, you become upset. You may blame yourself for his or her unhappiness, which creates the Earth Angel cycle of codependency, where your happiness is dependent upon another's. And since you can't control others' happiness, you feel unable to predict or control your own, as it's contingent upon someone else.

Earth Angels are usually "conflict-phobic," meaning that they fear arguments and confrontations. Angry people are the opposite of happy people to an Earth Angel. So if faced with such an individual, Earth Angels will shut down and usually comply with the other person's wishes, feeling at fault if someone is unhappy or angry. They are convinced they've failed in their mission to bring happiness to others. As a result, Earth Angels will do practically *anything* to keep the peace!

Their conflict phobia makes Earth Angels targets for manipulative people who take advantage of others' niceness. Before they learn their earthly lesson about holding boundaries, Earth Angels usually fall under the spell of narcissistic individuals who only care about their own needs. (We'll discuss this topic in depth throughout this book.)

Earth Angels find themselves in a bind because their life purpose is to bring peace to the world. They are lights sent from heaven to shine peace and happiness and lift others' consciousness and vibrations—so they're usually the world's kindest, nicest, and gentlest people! In fact, they pride themselves on being sweet in the roughest of situations (although Earth Angels do lose their tempers when pushed to their limit).

Earth Angels view themselves as tough, even though they're highly sensitive. They shoulder other people's burdens and rarely ask for help. If help is offered, they won't accept it. They're afraid of "bothering" anyone. An Earth Angel thinks: *If I allow this person to help me, I'm making him go to a lot of trouble, which might result in him feeling tired or sad. I don't want to inflict that on another person, so I'll just do everything myself.*

Because Earth Angels can see everyone's hidden potentials and inner light, they tend to overlook other people's hurtful behavior—especially toward *them*. An Earth Angel will make excuses about someone who's mistreating them, saying, "Oh, she didn't mean it . . . it wasn't that bad," or "He was just having a rough day." The person who's acting hurtfully doesn't need to expend any effort in justifying him- or herself, because the Earth Angel does it *for* him or her!

How are such people supposed to learn about the effects of their behavior if Earth Angels are constantly making excuses for them? How are others supposed to take responsibility for their lives, if Earth Angels are offering to do everything for them?

As an Earth Angel, you're here to bring more light into the world, not to enable people's egocentric behavior! By constantly giving in all of your relationships, you may suffer from symptoms of imbalance, including:

— **Resentment.** Feeling used for being nice, and not having the niceness reciprocated, you may find that the resentment builds up, becoming a toxic, acidic energy that sours you and can lead to health consequences.

— **Fatigue.** Constantly giving is draining on your time, energy, finances, and other resources. You may stay up late and get up early to have enough time to give to others.

— **Money issues.** Are you paying for everything? This is an unhealthy imbalance in your relationships.

— **Health issues.** You may develop serious health concerns from your energy imbalances. These can range from skin problems (repressed anger) to weight gain (protecting yourself with body fat) to throat ailments (fear of speaking up) to breast issues (nursing everyone until you're drained).

If you have high self-esteem, you'll choose relationships with nice people who won't take advantage of you. However, most Earth Angels are drawn to unhappy people who need "fixing." This gives them a sense of purpose.

You might meet truly nice people, but not notice or be attracted to them because they're already healed. So your heart beats faster when you meet unhappy or angry people, since they present a challenge. *I can make him happy,* you unconsciously decide.

Other people can sense that you're desperate for them to be happy. So they start to take advantage of you and depend upon you for their entertainment, support, and emotional well-being. And when they're unhappy (which is most of the time, because only *they* can give happiness to themselves . . . and we're *all* unhappy when we're taking advantage of someone else, or looking outside of ourselves for happiness), they blame *you!* And you then blame yourself, and your light dims.

Part of your life purpose is learning how to have healthy boundaries with others. It's about loving people in a way that's healthy, instead of "enabling" them.

><

$\mathcal{I}$NTRODUCTION

What Does It Mean to Be "Assertive"?

There's a lot of confusion and misunderstandings about the word *assertive*. Some people confuse assertiveness with aggression. It's no wonder they're afraid of being assertive!

Therefore it's very important that we define our terms so that we can have a mutual understanding of what we're talking about here.

A Definition of Assertiveness

Assertiveness means that you're aware of your feelings and opinions and that you state them to yourself and others in a way that respects other people's rights. An assertive person is kind, peaceful, and gentle yet never apologizes for his or her feelings, because feelings are to be honored and respected. Assertiveness is spiritually Divine, because it's a way of interacting that acknowledges that you are one and equal with others. Therefore, you have as much right to be happy as other people.

— **Assertiveness in personal relationships**: If you're assertive, you know that relationships are built upon revealing your true self. Otherwise you'll never feel loved, because the other person doesn't even know the real you! The only way to genuinely feel loved is to take the risk of being your true self and then find that you're accepted and cherished for who you really are.

— **Assertiveness in business**: In business settings, it's all about gaining respect. When you're assertive at work, you tell it like it is. You don't raise your voice or put anybody else down personally or attack others' opinions. You don't have to be tough or traditionally "masculine" to be assertive. In fact, assertiveness can be extremely gentle. An assertive businessperson speaks calmly and passionately at the same time.

— **Assertiveness in life-purpose situations**: As an Earth Angel, you have a very important life mission. You're here to speak up on behalf of those who can't speak for themselves (such as children, animals, oppressed people, and Mother Nature and the environment). You're here to help others hear and trust Divine messages. So this means you'll be called into doing work as a teacher, where you convey important information, either in a formal setting such as a classroom or as you meet people along the way.

As an Earth Angel, you're also expected to do advocacy or activism work. This means staying aware of what is going on in the world and making sure everyone has a voice. In practical terms this means that you'll sign petitions, speak out, spread awareness, go to meetings, contact your local representatives, volunteer, pray, and attend peaceful rallies.

What Assertiveness Is Not

Now let's contrast that assertive energy with aggression and other similar characteristics.

Aggression means that you care only for your own feelings and rights and not about the other person. Aggression is loud, angry, and ugly. An aggressive individual wants to wear down the other person's resolve by being imposing, threatening, and obnoxious until his or her demands are agreed to.

Of course, we all occasionally lose our tempers. And hopefully we learn from this every time it occurs. The learning can be about ways to deal with anger that don't involve storing it up until we become explosive.

Aggression is different from occasionally losing your cool. Aggression means that you're selfishly pushing your will upon another person. It means that you've decided that your rights are more important than someone else's. Earth Angels are much too sensitive to engage in this type of behavior for long. The Earth Angel knows that we are all one, with equal rights.

Passive-Aggression

Passive-aggression is often confused with assertiveness. The passive-aggressive response means that you're afraid of conflict, so you show your anger in ways that hurt other people but are so under-the-radar that you can't be blamed.

— **In business settings:** Passive-aggressive people sabotage the work assignment that they don't want to do. For example, a woman I know was given a task at work that she absolutely deplored. But she was afraid of saying no to her boss, so instead she made many mistakes while completing the task to ensure that she'd never be asked to do it again.

— **In personal relationships:** Examples of passive-aggression include withholding love or sex until you get your way, or saying something mean about your partner in public that you haven't had the courage to say directly to him or her in private.

Passivity

And then there's just plain old *passivity.* This means that you don't acknowledge your feelings to yourself or others. Being passive means that you have numbed your feelings so that you no longer care about yourself, others, or the issues in the world. Passive people have run away from responsibility and their emotions by "checking out" through drug use or other addictive behavior, spaciness, depression, isolation, or running from job to job or relationship to relationship.

— **In business settings:** Passive people go along with their bosses' whims and wishes without question. In life in general, passive people are like corks floating on the sea, without any control or opinions. They have dreams, but they never expect to realize them. Dreams are for "lucky, rich, or famous people." The passive person believes that fortunate people were born that way, without realizing that the same opportunities are available to everyone through determination and hard work.

— **In personal relationships:** Being passive means that you allow others to control what you do. This is often called "being a doormat." People who are passive frequently become depressed, in a state that is referred to in psychology as *learned helplessness*. It's almost as if your spirit has been beaten out of you. Fortunately, your soul is alive and well, and ready to be reignited.

Some people are passive because they're afraid of being seen for who they are. This usually stems from a childhood where they were teased or punished for speaking or acting up, or from a past life in which they were killed or tortured or faced some other painful outcome. While passive people desperately want to be effective in this world, they're afraid of taking that risk. So in my teaching and Angel Therapy work, I help them see that they *aren't* living in their childhood or that painful medieval life they remember—and that life is about taking risks!

Homework from Heaven

Occasionally I will meet people who will argue with me about their passivity. They'll tell me that they're being passive in relationships and in the world because they're using the Law of Attraction. Their argument is that what you think about comes into being, so they're only going to *think* about goodness and peace and happiness.

And it's wonderful to put your whole focus on the positive! But it's not enough. Covering negativity with positive affirmations is like throwing a new rug over a dirty floor. The dirt's still there!

If prayers and positive thoughts were enough, you and I could have just stayed in heaven and sent positive energy to the people here on Earth. When we truly pray (and don't just mouth the words), we always receive "homework from heaven," which are action steps we're Divinely guided to take.

Homework-from-heaven action steps include reading a book, making a call or driving across town, teaching others about a topic, starting a new project, and so forth.

The reason why we're in physical human bodies is because there's a need for our human voice, our human efforts, and our human action steps.

Think of the different archangels as the heavenly counterpart to this:

- **Archangel Michael** is constantly effecting his purpose of eradicating fear by taking angelic action steps. He uses his signature sword and peaceful warrior energy to clear away lower energies.

- **Archangel Ariel** is very active in helping heal and preserve the environment.

- And then there's **Archangel Gabriel**, whose actions involve delivering messages and encouraging human messengers such as writers, teachers, and artists.

These angels offer perfect examples of ways for us Earth Angels to take action. Sometimes we need to put up a fight like Archangel Michael. Sometimes we need to stand up for the environment like Archangel Ariel. And at other times we need to speak up like Archangel Gabriel. These are all very powerful action steps!

Sending light and love doesn't mean mouthing words and saying a quick prayer. It means going deep within yourself and calling upon the power of God and the universe to fill you up and then sending that power outward. This doesn't have to take a lot of time, but it does mean blocking out external distractions. So close your eyes and breathe deeply, and call upon the light and the love of the universe to build within you and strengthen your resolve.

PART I

ASSERTIVENESS BASICS

CHAPTER ONE

IT ALL BEGAN
WITH THE
ORIGINAL
TRAUMA

*B*efore you were born, you had an ideal life in heaven. (*Heaven* refers to a high-vibrational non-physical existence. It's where we live in between our physical lives.)

In heaven, there are no bills to pay, no urgent deadlines, and no stress. You spend your time helping earthly people and animals, learning how the universe works, and growing in your understanding and elevating your vibration.

On Earth, the ego rules the roost because the physical body demands to be fed, clothed, and sheltered. This sets up a system of competition where people maneuver to get their needs met. The belief is: *I better get mine before someone else does.* So there's a lot of rushing around, scurrying to compete and earn money.

Now let's take a deep breath and let all that energy go as we focus upon heaven. In contrast to Earth's materially competitive focus, in heaven every need is automatically met. There's no physical body, so there's no competition for food or jobs.

There's no competition in heaven, because there are no needs. No one needs money, houses, cars, prestige, or employment. So no one tricks or manipulates you. Why would they, when there's nothing to gain? Besides, all truth is palpable and apparent in heaven, so there's no way to deceive others.

In heaven, everyone feels supported and respected for who they are. Kindness and consideration prevail, and there's infinite patience. Everyone behaves lovingly toward everyone else, as most people have reached the spiritual realization of oneness, so they know that how they treat others is actually how they're treating themselves.

Imagine . . .

Take a moment to imagine feeling completely loved and honored. There's no sense of having to prove yourself. You know you're lovable, just as everyone is. Experience this warm feeling of complete love in your heart, and let that warmth radiate throughout your body.

Imagine what it's like to trust everyone you meet, and feel relaxed and safe in their presence. You know that all whom you encounter have their hearts open and are acutely aware of oneness. So they won't do anything mean, because they know that this would only be an act of meanness toward themselves.

Imagine being where everyone is happy and healthy. Where the sun always shines, and it's just the right temperature. Imagine flowers and birds and trees in a perpetual springtime. . . .

You're seeing and feeling <u>heaven.</u>

The Recruitment Process

So there you are in heaven, relaxing and doing your work and feeling so good because you are entirely loved. And then one day recruiters arrive, asking you to return to Earth for a very important mission that only you can fulfill. At first you balk at their request. After all, the last time you were on Earth, people weren't that nice to you.

You recall past lifetimes when you were also an Earth Angel. And throughout history, Earth Angels, with their spiritual gifts of healing and teaching, have often been misunderstood. In fact, there was at least one lifetime when you were accused of witchcraft because of your spiritual healing gifts. You were persecuted, and your death was not easy.

So when the recruiters are asking you to return to Earth, you're not excited about the prospect. You inquire whether you can simply send prayers and guidance to earthly people from your heavenly vantage point.

The recruiters bow their heads and sigh. They explain to you that people often don't listen to their guides or angels. They say that Earth Angels are needed in human bodies, because people only listen to other people.

The recruiters show you how you can benefit by going to Earth. After all, Earth gives you the opportunity to learn and grow and heal any fears that you held previously. On this plane you have the opportunity to feel deeply both physically and emotionally. You also have the experience of duality, where you get to encounter the darkness and the light.

Besides, the recruiters explain, they *need* you on Earth. They need you to guide people who aren't as aware and experienced as you are.

So reluctantly, you agree to come back to Earth in a human form. With the help of your guides and the recruiters, every part of your life is mapped out ahead of time. Of course you have freewill choices about everything, but the guides are very influential in urging you to balance your karma with certain people. So you agree to have them as your parents, friends, and partners. You've been with these souls in other lifetimes. And it's essential that you clear any unforgiveness, fear, or anger that you might harbor in those relationships. Spiritual growth also calls for you to take 100 percent responsibility for everything that you see, feel, and think.

The Original Trauma

After you're born, you look around as a baby for that unconditional love that you had in heaven. Your parents love you, but like all earthly humans, their hearts are partially closed. Your parents, like all people, have fears that block them from the full experience of love.

You immediately go into withdrawal, like an addict quitting drugs cold-turkey. *Where's the love? Where's the love?* is your panicked cry, as you desperately seek that delicious feeling of heavenly bliss and joy. Your parents do their best to keep you happy, but you unconsciously know that something's missing.

For your entire life, you seek that feeling of unconditional love. You meet someone and think, *This is it!* You believe that each new person is the source of the love you desperately seek.

Deep down, you remember how you felt in heaven. There, you felt completely accepted for who you are. You felt lighthearted, optimistic, carefree, and completely loved and loving.

Most of all, you felt safe. In heaven, there was no sense of stress, strain, or danger. Everyone was trustworthy, and no one wanted anything from you, except for you to be happy.

Doesn't that sound heavenly?

So you spend a lifetime looking for that sense of approval, safety, peace, and love. You may find that feeling temporarily in relationships, food, alcohol, or drugs. Some people encounter this bliss when they're in nature, exercising, having sex, shopping, or engaged in a creative process. For most, it's fleeting.

What's helpful to know is that we can never entirely replicate heaven's high vibrations in our earthly world of duality. We can come very close, and we can have pockets of moments where we're one with love. But it's unrealistic to think that we can maintain that state at all times.

The best you can do is to keep the doorway to heaven open in your heart. This allows you to have a continual warm feeling of love every day, no matter what's going on in your life or in the world.

In meditation one day, I heard and felt the presence of Archangel Michael. He explained the importance of enjoying life, no matter what's going on. He said that very often, we put our happiness in the future. We think that happiness is conditional, based upon certain achievements, such as earning enough money, accolades, or approval; losing weight; getting married; buying a new house; being published; or some other accomplishment. While those experiences can be very exciting and fulfilling, they still don't replicate that complete feeling of safety and approval that we have when we're in heaven.

You get close to those heavenly feelings when you're balancing giving and receiving. When you're only giving, you're excluding yourself from the sense that you deserve and need love, too. So it's a matter of focusing upon service and giving from your soul, and also giving to yourself.

Pure Giving

The only form of giving that leads to spiritual growth and true peace is when you give because you're guided to. Doing so because you feel guilty, sorry for someone, or obligated is giving from a place of fear. That means you'd be acting from your lower self, and the gift—whether it's time, money, help, advice, support, or love—would be tainted with the lower frequencies of that guilt, fear, or obligation energy.

As Earth Angels, we're here to give, help, and heal. And the *reason why we give* is the difference between creating a life of joy for ourselves and others . . . and living like a victim or martyr in misery:

- If you're giving because you hope that you'll be appreciated and loved for all that you do, you'll constantly feel disappointed that you're not getting as much in return as you gave. You'll also have an empty feeling that people love you for what you can do for them, instead of for who you are.

- If you're giving in order to keep someone from being angry with you, then you'll always feel nervous, like you have to walk on eggshells in case that person, despite your efforts, still decides to be upset with you.

- If you're giving because you hope that the person will help you in return, you'll always feel guilty that your true intentions were impure. You'll also feel hurt when the other person doesn't reciprocate.

Only give because you truly are happy to do so. In that experience, you'll find your heavenly bliss. In fact, a good rule to live by is:

Never do anything unless you want to.
Either don't do the action, or go meditate and pray until you can shift your mind-set to one of happiness toward it.

CHAPTER TWO

HOW
TO BE
ASSERTIVE

As a peace-loving, gentle person, you may have learned to avoid conflict at all costs. You just go along with someone's bad idea rather than stand up to him or her and risk an argument. This style of living gives you a sense of control over your life, because deep down *you* know you're not really agreeing with the person. It's as if you're leading two lives: one on the surface, with your behavior; and the other beneath, with your true feelings and opinions.

In some cases, Earth Angels have numbed themselves so much in order to cooperate with others that they've completely disconnected from their own opinions. They don't know how they feel or what they think about anything, because they're so accustomed to being *told* what to do, feel, and think. Sometimes, tragically, this is because of an abusive situation where they fear for their physical safety, so they comply with their abusers' wishes in order to survive.

Still other Earth Angels are conflict-phobic because they're shy and don't want to call attention to themselves. They'd rather remain invisible, so they almost never speak up for themselves. And when they *do*, people don't hear or notice them.

The trouble with these coping styles is that if you don't let people know how you feel, they'll incorrectly assume that everything's okay. *People won't know how you really feel or think unless you tell them.*

In addition, assertiveness means that you're clear, honest, and direct with others. Hinting at how you feel and hoping the other person gets the hint never works. This is a guarantee that you'll always feel ignored and misunderstood. Instead of hinting, you have to clearly communicate your feelings.

You may worry that if you're truthful, people will leave you. But the truth is that *you'll* be the one to leave, if you don't muster up the courage to be honest. If you don't tell the other person how you really feel, the relationship will be unbalanced and unhealthy, and you—as a highly sensitive person—won't want to stay.

Being conflict-phobic can also block you from fulfilling the very important mission you were born to do! In order to fulfill your lightwork, you need to reawaken and own your power!

If this sounds frightening or dangerous, please stay with me anyway. The fear is coming from your ego and past experiences. Fortunately, it isn't based upon reality as it relates to your future or your Divine mission.

Remember that if the earth were perfect, you and I wouldn't be needed here in physical form. We could have just stayed in heaven and sent prayers to everyone. But humans rarely hear their angels, or if they do, they wrestle with self-doubts. So we were sent to Earth to speak up and take other actions to enact God's will of peace. Being passive isn't in our job description.

Peace is our mission. And being peaceful is very different from being passive.

The Superwoman/Superman Syndrome of Earth Angels

As an Earth Angel, you possess certain "superpowers." Some Earth Angels have a superpower of invisibility, for instance. This means that they can slip in and out of places and situations relatively unnoticed. Of course, the downside to having an invisibility superpower is that you're often ignored by waiters and waitresses, and even loved ones.

What's Your Superpower?

Every Earth Angel has something amazing that he or she is good at. Here are a few examples of Earth Angel superpowers:

- Healing
- Manifesting
- Breaking* or fixing electronics

---

* If you break every watch, computer, and radio you come near, then your life purpose is to thwart destructive electronics, such as weapons or anything that harms people, animals, or the environment.

- Animal communication

- Miraculous gardening abilities

- Weather magic

- Knowing instantly whether someone is being honest

- Foreseeing the future

There are many other superpowers, too. Spend time pondering what yours is. Observe yourself with others or out in nature and notice what comes very easily and magically to you. That's your superpower!

Your superpower is a skill that you brought from heaven to help with your life mission. For example, if you can easily hear the voices of animals talking, then your life purpose involves animal communication. If you have a talent for predicting or influencing the weather, your purpose involves protecting people from major storms.

Taking Off Your Cape

Even superheroes need a day off. As Earth Angels, we're inordinately strong emotionally and physically. We're used to being the helpers in relationships, and the ones who come to everyone's rescue.

But sometimes our superpowers can confuse us. We may say yes to every request for help, without first meditating on how that new duty will impact our already-full schedule.

Even though you have broad shoulders and a big heart, your assertiveness training involves learning to say no, especially to unreasonable demands upon your time.

After all, time is your greatest resource in putting your life purpose into action. For example, if you're destined to become a healer in private practice and are intending to make this happen, you'll need to devote many hours to your clients. That means that any hours spent doing an activity purely because of guilt, out of obligation, or because you were bullied into it will be time taken away from your clients. That time spent doing something meaningless could be better directed toward healing someone—or even saving his or her life.

So if you're reluctant to say no to time and energy drains, then do it for your clients!

How to Stand Up for Yourself

When confronted with any form of danger, every living creature defends itself. This is a hardwired response built into every physical being to guarantee its survival. So it's okay to acknowledge to yourself that *you* have a defense mechanism.

This doesn't make you less spiritual or less angelic in any way. Again, think of warrior angels such as Archangel Michael with his sword and his armor, signifying that even the most peaceful angels have to sometimes go to battle. And there's a feminine equivalent to Archangel Michael's archetype within every woman. Research stories of strong warrior women, like Joan of Arc or the suffragettes.

When someone says or does something that stirs a reaction in you, it's very important to acknowledge your thoughts and feelings to yourself. Perhaps you notice that your stomach muscles tighten; you perspire; or you become flush with anger, rage, or even embarrassment. If at all possible, walk away from the situation, even if you have to excuse yourself to go to the restroom. This moment away helps calm down your physiological reactions. Otherwise, you may act impulsively and say things that you later regret.

While you're alone, have an honest conversation with yourself. Begin by noticing how you feel physically. Is your heart racing, is your breathing shallow, or are your thoughts explosive? Any of these reactions can show that the other person has triggered anxiety within you.

This anxiety response is also called *fight or flight*. It's an instinctual response to danger. When there's danger, your instincts spur you into either fighting or running away (that is, *flight*).

While you're by yourself and meditating, it's a good idea to pray for guidance, support, and peace. You want to be honest with yourself and with others, but you don't want to blow situations out of proportion. Nor do you want to engender hard feelings.

❖—❖

Whenever we avoid conflict by keeping our feelings to ourselves, we do ourselves and others a disservice. This is a form of dishonesty and manipulation. We're trying to control the other person's reactions by controlling what we tell them.

So that means you're being controlling if someone asks you if you're upset and you say that you aren't when you really are. You're trying to keep him or her from being angry with you or from starting an argument with you. Or, you're holding your feelings inside to prevent the other person from seeing that you are hurt.

Now, that doesn't mean you have to go to the other extreme and bulldoze the other person with the blunt truth. There's an in-between way to handle conflict that's just right and very healthy and honest. After you've collected your thoughts and feelings, go to the person and say this magical phrase: "I'd like to clear some things with you."

This nonthreatening phrase keeps communication open because the other person doesn't feel accused. Start by taking a deep breath and silently praying for strength and a clear mind. Even though your heart may be racing and you might even be perspiring, know that anytime you do something for the first time, you'll feel intimidated or afraid. Each time you practice a new behavior, it becomes easier and more natural.

Look the other person in the eye and say to him or her from your heart and without apology: "I really care about our relationship, so I need to share my feelings in order for us to clear them."

Now, the other person *may* feel threatened by this and might immediately become defensive or even argumentative. Don't let this throw you, unless the other person becomes verbally or physically abusive.

(Don't try to negotiate with an abusive person, especially if he or she intoxicated. If abuse occurs, leave immediately and seek appropriate support or protection.)

In most situations, others will be open to hearing you. During your discussion, it's vital that you own your feelings. This means: don't use blaming or shaming words. Even if you *do* blame them, *saying* that you do will shut down all further communication.

Use phrases such as *I feel, I felt,* and *to me.* This way, you're not poking and prodding at the other person with accusatory phrases, and inadvertently provoking their defensiveness.

Do your best to keep your cool while talking about and owning your feelings. If you start to cry, let yourself be real. The same with anger: allow yourself to be authentic, but don't act on this emotion, such as by yelling or calling names. Also, please don't put *yourself* down in any way.

Don't diminish, disparage, or apologize for your feelings . . . *ever!* Remember: You have a right to your feelings, even if other people don't understand or agree with them! Your feelings are your signals of deep truths inside of you. They're the language of your soul, and they need you to listen to them.

After you've talked about your feelings, allow the other person to explain his or her own. There are always two sides to every story. However, notice your gut feelings while you're listening. If you get an uneasy feeling that the other person is covering his or her tracks or being dishonest with you, then note that—because he or she probably *is.*

As your assertiveness level grows stronger, you'll have the courage to say to a person who's lying to you, "I don't believe what you're saying," or something equivalent. But for now, just notice that you get the feeling that he or she is being dishonest, manipulative, or defensive.

This isn't the kind of person you want to spend much time with. Those are toxic behavior patterns that permeate all of that individual's relationships.

If the other person starts blaming you or is defensive, the conversation will go in an unproductive direction. Blaming is a key symptom of the ego's fears about being exposed. As long as one or both of you are involved in blaming, nothing will get resolved.

Toxic relationships will pull you down every time. You don't need to have one when there are so many *non*toxic potential friends and partners available. Never believe you have to settle for an unhealthy relationship. You don't.

Boundaries

A boundary is your limit, which no one can overstep or violate. No matter who the other person is or how much you love him or her, your boundary is something that he or she is not allowed to breach.

For instance, I have boundaries in all of my relationships that dictate that you must treat me with respect. I, in turn, will treat you with respect. This is a non-negotiable boundary for me, and if anyone violates this and is disrespectful toward me, I will try to clear the energy by discussing my feelings and boundaries, and then listening to the other person. If he or she continues to be disrespectful toward me, the relationship is over, without any guilt on my part. I still love the person, but because of the behavior overstepping my firm boundary, I no longer have contact with him or her. Boundaries are a necessary part of self-care, just like washing your hair or wearing shoes to protect your feet. They are healthy, normal, and necessary.

Every relationship has issues and negotiations about each person's personal boundaries. So it's not *whether* you have conflict, but *how you deal with conflict* that matters for a long-term relationship.

Personal boundaries include how much . . .

- . . . body space and distance from other people you need.

- . . . time alone you prefer.

- . . . affection and romance you require.

- . . . you need to hear words of affection.

- . . . you need your personal items to be left alone and untouched by others.

- . . . importance you attach to honesty, reliability, and sobriety within the relationship.

- . . . financial equality and fairness matter to you. [. . . and so forth.]

Part of being an assertive Earth Angel is learning how to have the strength and the courage to maintain your boundaries. It can get exhausting when it feels like other people are trying to step all over them. It might wear you down, and you start to think, *Does this really matter?* Well, it does!

Your inner self relies upon your outer self for caretaking. You might say that your inner self is like a little child you're nurturing. That means that if it's tired or needs to play, your outer self should honor this and not push your inner self beyond its limits.

Even though the other person may be disappointed or even angry when you say no, believe me when I tell you that he or she *does* understand. Remember that the other person is human, too, and knows what limitations are like. Even if your refusal comes as a disappointment, deep down he or she will respect you for it!

When you say no, you're modeling healthy behavior for others. Part of the reason why they may react angrily toward you is because it's never occurred to them that *they* could say no to unreasonable demands put upon their own time!

So when you do something that people haven't seen you do previously—like saying no—they may be surprised. They may take your refusal personally, and it's okay for you to briefly explain that this isn't anything personal and has to do with you maintaining clear boundaries with respect to your schedule.

Don't feel like you have to explain why you're saying no, though. The more you explain why, the more leverage the other person has, which he or she can use to manipulate you into changing that *no* into a *yes*.

Boundaries mean that you teach people what you will and won't accept in the relationship. They can be a lot of work, but that's what it takes to build a healthy relationship with yourself and others.

Respect your right to schedule your time. Don't allow others to dictate your schedule to you. For instance, you have the right to not answer the phone or doorbell when it rings, and to not feel obligated to immediately answer e-mails or social-media posts. If someone asks you to drop everything to drive him or her across town, you have the right to say no. It's like the adage "Lack of planning on your part does not constitute an emergency on my part." We must overcome impulsive rescuing tendencies, unless it's an actual emergency and we feel internally guided to help.

Source Is the Only Source

A lot of people use guilt to manipulate others into getting their way. They also include flattery mixed with guilt. So, as an example, they'll say, "Only *you* can help me; and if you don't help me, there will be horrible consequences for me."

As a sensitive Earth Angel, you don't want anyone to suffer, so you allow the other person's words to manipulate and control you. Then you feel weak and used, as well as resentful and angry. Add to this the frustration that arises because you've backtracked on your promise to take excellent care of yourself . . . and you've got a heap of toxic energies inside your mind, emotions, and body.

It's so important to remind yourself that every person has the same Source: *God.* Those who play with your emotions to get their way are creations of God, just like you and everyone else. You're not their God, nor are you their Source. So, allow Source God to be each person's caretaker. Pray for guidance about how you can truly help others gain strength and be self-sufficient.

Of course, there will be instances where you're acting as an Earth Angel and bringing forth God's help through your efforts. But those instances are clearly guided by love, not by guilt.

If you're giving because of guilt, it's not true or pure giving, as was discussed in the previous chapter. Your gift out of guilt is tainted with toxic energies.

Healthy Boundaries

Boundaries are a form of self-care. When you uphold your boundaries, meaning that you don't allow others to manipulate, guilt, or control you, your inner self applauds and thanks you.

Your self-esteem and confidence increase whenever you successfully stand up for yourself.

Now, by "stand up for yourself," I don't mean that you're aggressively pronouncing judgments over others. Remember that assertiveness upholds *everyone's* rights: yours and those of the other person involved. When you maintain your boundaries and say no with grace, love, and firmness, you teach people how to handle boundaries.

You're not their Source; God is! If you make yourself their Source, then how will they ever learn to support themselves and grow?

When I was first teaching angel courses, I made time to sit down personally one-on-one with each student. During these individual sessions, I'd tune in to the student's angels and answer all of the questions that he or she had. And then I'd go home and be ill and tired for two to three days after the workshop; I had allowed myself to become drained, under the misguided notion that *I* was the one to help and serve all these students.

After that, I realized that I wasn't doing myself or them any favors by being so accessible. I realized that it was important for me to model good healthy boundaries to my students, many of whom were in training to become spiritual teachers themselves. I needed to teach each student how to access Divine guidance and answers for him- or herself, instead of needing to go through me or another person.

So, in my teaching I began emphasizing how to receive clear angel messages for yourself. I also created defined breaks in the schedule for the course, during which I wouldn't allow anyone to ask me questions. When questioned during my break, I'd say: "Other people may want to hear the answer to this question, so let's save it for when we're all back together." I'd also tell students that I was in a human body that needed rest and recharging.

I knew that by taking a break, I'd be a more effective and higher-energy teacher. I'd also be happier, which is a very important quality in a teacher. I've always told my students that it's beneficial to take lots of different classes, as long as the teacher is a happy person. A happy teacher teaches other people how to be happy, both directly and by role-modeling happiness. And happiness is the most important thing anyone can teach!

In addition, when you exercise strong and healthy boundaries as a parent, you teach your children how to do the same. Don't you want your children to grow up learning to respect themselves, their time, and their energy levels? Of course you do! Well, so too does God want this for you and everyone else!

Affirm often: "I think I can; therefore I can!"

Plenty of people come to me and argue in favor of their limitations. They forcefully tell me why they can't enact the positive steps that their angels are guiding them to take. They imply that they're somehow exceptional and are being blocked or thwarted from their dreams. Everyone else gets cut a break, but they're very special victims in their own minds.

If they would put half the energy they expend arguing for what they *can't* do toward arguing in favor of what they *can* do, then they would be well on their way to living their dream lives!

Benefits of Boundaries

When you exercise your boundaries and learn to say no, you have more free time to devote to your passions and priorities, instead of feeling like you have to steal away moments to write that article, take that class, read that book, learn to play that musical instrument, start that new business, practice your healing skills . . . and so forth.

Boundaries give you a healthier and happier mind and a higher energy level, because you're no longer fixated on the thought that people have taken advantage of you. When you feel resentful, you obsessively think about the other person's inconsiderate behavior toward you. This type of thought pattern, if left unchecked, can lead to depression, anxiety, addictions, relationship issues, loneliness, fearfulness, and other toxic results.

CHAPTER THREE

NO MORE RESCUING:

BOUNDARIES WITHOUT GUILT or FEAR

*E*arth Angels think that rescuing is a normal part of all relationships. They see themselves as strong and able to manifest endless resources—which is an accurate description, because they've learned how to tap into Source for energy and supply.

Earth Angels are so empathetic that they can feel everyone's emotions, especially the painful ones. In fact, many Earth Angels have difficulty distinguishing their own feelings from other people's.

The combination of Earth Angels being able to feel other people's pain plus their desire for everyone to be happy makes them natural rescuers.

Rescuing is a beautiful thing to do if you're a fire-fighter or medical first responder, or in any situation where the person is unable to help him- or herself. But rescuing people who could dig themselves out of their own jams is where Earth Angels get into trouble.

When an Earth Angel steps in and rescues someone who's capable of rescuing him- or herself, this is called *enabling.* It means that you're taking away someone's opportunity to grow and learn.

An example would be a mother who still does her teenage son's laundry and cleans up his room and makes his bed when he's quite capable of doing all this himself. He would also *benefit* by learning how to take care of his environment.

Or think of the parents who complete their child's science project, even though the child would learn new skills by working on it alone with minimal adult supervision.

Some Earth Angels rescue strangers. They meet a new person whom they pity, and they offer outrageous help, including opening their house to a recent acquaintance to live in rent-free, loaning or giving money to an individual whom they barely know, spending hours on the phone offering advice, or driving a virtual stranger to appointments.

Rescuers believe it's their job to fix others, and they believe that they're uniquely qualified to do so. If *they* don't help, no one else can! This gives them a sense of meaning and purpose, and also can feed into egocentric feelings of specialness.

In addition, rescuing allows you to focus more on other people's problems than on your own (deflecting your energy away from fixing your own life).

Professional Victims Beware of "professional victims." Earth Angels have a compulsion to save people and so are a lock-and-key with those who exploit them, and who insist upon constantly being rescued. Although you know that everyone is a child of God, you must also acknowledge that some people choose to live disconnected from God's guidance. They take advantage of others, including nice people like you.

Professional victims will make you feel flattered and special, as they explain that you're their only hope. They've singled you out especially because God "told" them that you'd fix everything for them. So you take a deep breath, agree to help them, and think, *I'll figure out how I can help as I go along,* since you have no idea what to do at the time. You also wonder how you'll keep your own life in balance while taking on the Herculean task of rescuing yet another person.

So you do your best to lend a hand, but the professional victim lets you know that your help doesn't come quickly enough or isn't good enough. Surely there's *more* you can give to this poor victim? Somewhere along the line, you reach a breaking point or a loved one points out that your rescuing behavior is unhealthy.

When you stop rescuing professional victims, they get angry. Very angry. And they then begin attacking you with verbal threats, rude posts on your social-media page, or harassing phone messages. In fact, *while* you're rescuing them, they attack you for not doing a good enough job of it. You're never doing enough for them. If they're unhappy, professional victims will say that it's your fault.

So the next time you get the compulsion to rescue someone, pray for guidance first. Professional victims have endless drama and bottomless-pit needs that can never be filled. They're *ungrateful* for the help they get, and in fact they criticize it.

You'll never feel satisfaction while rescuing a professional victim, because they intend to suck and drain you dry. (We'll talk more about how to identify and handle these toxic relationships in Part II.)

Rescuing Addiction

Addictions are always an attempt to fill an inner emotional emptiness with something outside of ourselves. The addiction momentarily makes us experience those delicious feelings of safety, love, and peace—just as we did prior to the original trauma (see Chapter 1).

You feel like a hero when you rescue someone, which is a sensation that temporarily boosts your self-esteem. This feeling is very strong if you believe, *Only I can help him. He's counting on me!*

Now is it really true that you're the only one who can rescue the person? What are some alternatives for him if you *weren't* available to rescue him? Please be honest with yourself about the answers to these questions.

You become addicted to rescuing when there's a pattern across several relationships where you're the clear rescuer and the other person is a victim in need of rescuing. *Rescue addiction* has the classic hallmarks shared with other addictions: You start to depend upon the behavior in order to feel whole, happy, or important. You conduct rescuing impulsively by immediately saying "I'll do it!" without first considering alternatives or the aftermath.

The rescue addiction, like any addiction, leads to messy consequences. Soon after enlisting yourself to rescue someone, you start to experience familiar feelings creeping in: being overwhelmed with too much to do; resenting that no one else is helping; feeling unappreciated by those you're helping; wishing you were instead spending time on a personally meaningful project; and feeling guilty because you're conflicted about rescuing the person. These feelings are intensified even more if the person you're rescuing begins to make additional demands on your time or other resources.

So, what's wrong with rescuing? *A lot!* If you rescue others, you rob them of the chance to develop problem-solving skills. You also give people a safety net to get entangled in another crisis, because they know that they can depend upon you to bail them out. In addition, the addiction is caustic to your self-esteem because you don't have a healthy, real relationship with those whom you rescue. Instead, the relationship makes you feel that you're only loved for what you can do for others, instead of being loved for who you are. That's a lonely feeling that leads to the downward spiral of low self-worth.

Volunteering for Committees

Volunteer service is God's work, in that volunteers fulfill much-needed roles in communities. But there's a balance some Earth Angels need help achieving!

It's one thing to volunteer to assist part-time with a project that's dear to your heart. But it's another thing to feel railroaded and pressured to join multiple committees in which you have no interest.

Unless you're sure that the volunteer work brings you joy, skip it. You're not truly giving unless you're giving from a place of love. There are plenty of volunteer positions available that are aligned with your personal passions and natural interests.

Similar to this are committees at your job that are unpaid and which you're pressured to join. Remember that it's okay to say no to activities for which you don't have the extra time. As long as you're doing your regular job well, you'll be appreciated. And if you're not appreciated at work, it's time to dust off your résumé and look for a position where you will be!

Discernment, Not Judgment

Earth Angels pride themselves on being nonjudgmental. That's why it's important for them to develop a sense of *discernment* instead.

Discernment operates off of the Law of Attraction. It says: *I am attracted to this; I am not attracted to that.* For example, discernment might say that you're not drawn to something. Judgment, on the other hand, labels everything as either being good or bad. So it's more intellectual in its scope. With judgment, you'd say: *This person is bad. That person is good.* With discernment, the Law of Attraction would say: *I am attracted to this person. I am not attracted to that person.*

With discernment, you're honest with yourself about how you feel in the presence of another person or situation. You don't try to rationalize your feelings. You don't downplay them. You listen to and honor them with discernment!

Be discerning about whom you hang out with, because those folks will influence your energy and experiences in life. Yes, you can see the good in everyone, but if a relationship is toxic, it can pull you way down.

For example, I used to belong to a meditation group in which we took turns leading the meditation and offering a brief teaching each week. The group was harmonious, sweet, uplifting, and supportive. Then one day, a self-proclaimed atheist said he wanted to join our group. Being an openhearted, "we love everyone" type of group, we had a discussion and decided to allow him in. That's when trouble started, as the man began playing devil's advocate to everything we said and arguing every point. Our meditation group became unpleasant, and we all stopped meeting within one month of his joining.

So sometimes, it's for the greatest good of all concerned if you say no to someone entering your life.

CHAPTER FOUR

HOW TO BE
NICE AND LOVING,
WITHOUT BEING A
PUSHOVER

*E*arth Angels are nice because they're very sensitive to how energies affect other people. They treat others as they'd wish to be treated, very much living by the Golden Rule.

Earth Angels see the best in others and expect the best in return. Oh, if only the world really worked that way!

The three-dimensional physical world contains the ego, and the ego prevails for the majority of people, who aren't aware of the path of true happiness from living in the higher self.

Now, this doesn't mean that Earth Angels need to lower their standards and try to fit into the lowest common denominator of rude or ego-based behavior. But it does require Earth Angels to be aware of ego energy when it shows up.

If you have been taken advantage of repeatedly for being a nice person, then please pay extra attention to this chapter.

The ego energy is all about "me" and "I": *What is in it for me?* and *What can I get out of this?*

That's why self-centered people are called *egocentric* or *egotistical.*

Therefore, it's important to take some time when you're with someone to tune in and be very aware of how your body feels in that person's presence. Your body is one of the most accurate divination tools on this physical plane. It is a crystal that resonates with energy vibrations.

So when you meet someone, rather than worrying, *Does she like me? Am I good enough?* and posing these sorts of self-doubting questions, instead listen to what your body says. Notice:

- *Do I feel drained of energy when I'm around this person?*

- *Does my stomach tighten with defensiveness, bracing myself against some danger?*

- *Do I feel myself backing away from this person or wanting to leave her presence?*

- *Is there a sense that I'm the only one giving in this relationship?*

- *Does it feel like the other person is all about taking?*

- *Does the other person joke or brag about how much she gets away with or takes advantage of others?*

- *After being with this person, do I feel tired or depressed or anxious?*

So when you encounter a person who's ego-focused, you'll feel a draining sensation in your body, because your energy *is* literally being drained. You're also being scanned energetically by the egocentric person, who's assessing what she can take from you.

What egocentric people want to take from you can vary. They may be looking for simple things such as a listening ear or kind words. Most Earth Angels don't feel taken advantage of for giving these things, unless it becomes a one-sided relationship where you're the only one giving the compliments and doing the listening, and the other person never says anything nice to you, nor do they care enough to be your sounding board.

To find a person who isn't egocentric, you'll need to hold the intention of meeting other Earth Angels and givers . . . or those who have been working to develop self-awareness, and who have come to the realization that the path to true happiness is through balancing giving and receiving.

Relationships are synergistic. You can be as nice as an angel in heaven, but unless you're with someone who honors and respects your niceness, you'll tend to be taken advantage of by those who are egocentric.

If someone's egocentric, don't worry whether or not he or she likes you. Egocentric people are incapable of liking anyone, because their hearts are closed. They don't even like themselves.

When you get a sense that someone's a "taker," pull back your energy and don't try so hard. He or she is not worthy of your time or friendship, and you'll end up "breaking up" anyway when you get tired of being taken advantage of. You have a limited amount of time here on Earth, and it's best to spend it on someone who'll appreciate being helped.

Egocentric people see help from others as threatening to their egos, because it means they're "weak" if they accept it. They also see receiving help as "winning" in their endless game of taking as much as they can without giving anything in return.

When dealing with an egocentric person, it's not about getting his or her approval through being nice. It's impossible to get the approval of those who are only concerned about themselves. Instead, focus on being loving and on respecting yourself.

With all assertive encounters, your goal isn't to change the other person. Your intention is to be honest and authentic, and take good care of yourself and treat other people with respect.

Realness and Respect

If you were raised on platitudes like "If you can't say anything nice, don't say anything at all," you may mistake this wisdom as a directive to be "phony nice." There's a real difference between discerning when to hold your tongue and keep yourself from saying something hurtful versus faking a smile and pretending to laugh.

Many Earth Angels are nice because that's their way of manipulating and controlling the reactions of others.

And that's egocentric, too! Niceness that comes from fear that the other person may leave you or not like you unless you're super-sweet isn't a true gift to anyone.

Even the coldest and most unaware people have enough sensitivity to notice when someone's faking it. When selfish or egocentric people spot someone faking niceness, they think, *This person's trying too hard to act nice. She must want something from me. So I will take advantage of her first, before she can do the same to me!*

So, being "phony nice" makes you vulnerable to those who are looking for an easy take. In this dance, you're both being insincere. You, as the Earth Angel, exercise your power when you're your authentic self.

Every day, practice taking off the false-self mask of faking a smile when you don't feel like smiling. Daily, practice saying at least one sentence aloud that describes how you actually feel, even if you're afraid of others' reactions. With practice, you'll gain confidence and security in being your true self.

Instead of trying to make other people "like" you, you would be better off holding the intention to gain self-respect and the respect of others. "Respect" means that someone believes in you as a responsible, trustworthy, and real person. Respect and trust go hand in hand.

If you pretend to be happy when you're not, other people won't trust you, because they'll wonder in what other ways you're being phony. If you force a smile or laugh, others won't respect you, because phoniness shows that you don't respect yourself.

Everyone feels the whole rainbow of human emotions, and you're no exception. There will be times when you'll be really angry, and it's okay to let others know it as long as you don't hurl toxic anger energy their way.

There will be times when you'll be hurt, depressed, confused, silly, and every other color of emotion that exists. There will be occasions when you'll disagree with your boss or another authority figure.

The assertive Earth Angel's facial expression and body language match exactly with how she thinks and feels. She doesn't try to project a façade of coolness or happiness. She maintains respect for herself and others. She doesn't blame others for her feelings, but she is honest if she's upset with someone's behavior.

The assertive Earth Angel realizes that relationships are a series of negotiations between two people who may have style differences. By talking openly and respecting each other's feelings and opinions, both can have their needs met and enjoy a healthy, long-term relationship.

><

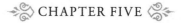

CHAPTER FIVE

COMMUNICATION
SKILLS FOR
EARTH ANGELS

*Y*our heightened sensitivity means that you feel others' reactions to what you say. So, your communication style differs from people of average sensitivity levels. In this chapter, we will look at some of those differences.

Talking in Incomplete Sentences

Earth Angels often worry that they're bothering other people. They rush through the words they're using so they don't take up other people's time. Or they skip over details about the topic they're discussing, either because they're trying to keep their side of the conversation brief . . . or because of the belief that others are as psychic as they are, with the assumption that they will know what they're talking about. Sometimes ungrounded Earth Angels talk in incomplete sentences that make no sense to anyone. And other Earth Angels use New Age jargon that "normal" people can't understand. ("What's a chakra?" they may ask with puzzlement.)

Other people become frustrated because they don't understand what you're trying to get across. This sets up miscommunications, which can lead to hurt feelings and other problems. So the first step for Earth Angels is to slow down and communicate enough information so the other person knows clearly what you're trying to convey. However, the opposite extreme of talking too much and dominating the conversation is also a communication trap that many Earth Angels fall into.

Talking nonstop comes from wanting to please—and get attention and acknowledgment from—others. If you tune in to people's eyes while you're talking with them, you'll know if they're engaged in the conversation with you. If you notice their eyes wandering or glazing over, this is a sign that you've lost communication with them. This can happen because of the other person's toxic behavioral patterns, such as narcissism or one-sided friendship. Or, it could be because he or she doesn't understand what you're talking about, or you're talking so much that he or she lost interest in connecting with you.

Some of these communication issues occur because Earth Angels are so sensitive to chemicals. So they can become overstimulated from caffeine or sugar, and have a motormouth in which they talk and talk and talk without realizing it. If that sounds like you, it's time to cut back on caffeine and sugar. Substitute natural stimulants such as rosehips tea or peppermint tea for these two chemicals.

It's also important to ground yourself, especially in business settings or while talking with "normal" people. Take a deep breath and touch your feet, or walk on grass or soil to ground yourself. Keep your conversations as down-to-earth and practical as possible. Save your philosophical discussions for ears that can hear these high-level topics.

Repeating Phrases

Earth Angels sometimes repeat themselves out of anxiety as well. One of the hallmark phrases that Earth Angels use is: "I'm sorry."

Earth Angels apologize continually, as if they are apologizing for their own existence. This again is because they're not accustomed to having a physical body. They realize that their bodies are taking up space and using resources, and they remember fondly the days when they were celestial angels who could help people without having any sort of physical interference.

The trouble with apologizing is that it's inappropriate and detracts from intelligent conversations. It's also an unconscious habit, which needs to come to the level of consciousness so that you can heal it and let it go. One way to do so is to create a pact with another Earth Angel friend of yours. Promise each other that you will gently point out when the other one is apologizing. This really works, as long as you're both kind to each other because you remember you are both highly sensitive to perceived criticism.

Earth Angels also tend to say "Thank you" repeatedly, especially if someone is doing them a favor. This is a sign of the Earth Angels' feelings of undeserving, and fear that they're taking up someone else's time and bothering him or her.

This, again, is because you're not accustomed to having a physical body, and you're also not used to allowing others to help you. When you were a celestial angel, you were the one doing all of the giving. But once you take on a physical body, you become part of the polarities of giving and receiving. So, while it is appropriate to offer your gratitude for someone's help, please be aware that it is unnatural, unnecessary, and ultimately annoying if you repeatedly thank the person.

Another oft-repeated phrase is the question "Are you mad at me?" Earth Angels take everything very personally, including another person's silence or need for space. If Earth Angels feel someone pulling back in the relationship, their first impulse is to chase after him or her and get reassurance that they're still loved and that the other person isn't upset with them.

This action always backfires, unless you are with a highly sensitive person who has compassion for your insecurities. In normal circumstances, though, when you repeatedly ask others if they're mad at you, you can actually push them *into* being angry with you.

So, if you're feeling insecure about your relationship, your best action is to sit down with the other person and say, "Do we need to clear anything? Are we okay?" And then be quiet and let the other person talk. Most of the time, people won't have any idea what you're talking about, because they're not mad at you at all. They will explain that they have their own issues, which are distracting them from their relationship with you.

If you feel you are being neglected in your relationship or your needs are not being met, you'll have to be very clear about this boundary and expectation with the other person. Relay this in an adult, assertive way, and not as a child begging for a scrap of attention. You need to respect yourself and your needs, and you deserve to be in a relationship where they're met!

Trying Too Hard

When you're communicating, don't try too hard to get other people to like you or to be impressed with you. Others can sense the energy of someone who is trying too hard. That energy is always repelling to people and pushes them away. No one likes to be coerced into anything, including being pushed into liking someone. A person who normally would be happy to be with you may think that something is wrong with you that you need to convince him or her to like you. This is especially true in heterosexual romantic relationships, where the man tends to like to do the pursuing and wooing. Let him come after you! Not the other way around.

Respect Yourself as You Respect Others

Don't talk "up" to people, as if you see them as an authority figure or have them on a pedestal and hold them superior to you. If you have a great deal of respect for someone or he or she is a celebrity, talk to him or her as if to a regular person. The Golden Rule of doing unto others as you would have them do unto you applies perfectly to conversations. You don't want anyone to make a fuss about you, and neither do other people (unless they are narcissists, and you don't want to be involved in that type of relationship anyway).

Complaining

Do you tend to complain a lot? If you do, you may be pushing people away. Those who complain come across as whining children, who see themselves as victims who have given away their power to others. You are neither a victim nor a little child. As an adult, you can make choices to change your life.

When you complain, are you looking for sympathy or solutions? The honest answer to this question can help reveal hidden fears of which you were unaware.

Complaining is an unconscious communication habit. It's a negative affirmation that draws to you the very thing you're complaining about. It does nothing to help improve your situation. So, instead of complaining, get to work on changing your life for the better!

-⋄—⋄-

In conversation, be real and authentic. Speak in enough detail that other people know what you're talking about. Don't start a conversation in the middle of a thought or assume that other people will psychically understand everything you've been thinking about.

Breathe while you're talking, and allow the other person to have space to reply. Be a good listener, and pay attention to what the other person is saying. Above all, though, listen to your own feelings as you're having a conversation. Because the most important conversations that you'll ever have are with your true self and with God.

CHAPTER SIX

GETTING RID OF GUILT AND WORRY

*T*wo emotions that are commonly experienced by Earth Angels are guilt and worry, and in this chapter, we'll examine each in turn.

Guilt

Guilt occurs for several reasons:

- You're engaging in an action that doesn't accord with your beliefs and morals.

- You believe you're not doing enough or haven't done enough.

- You believe that you should make everyone happy. When someone's unhappy, you blame yourself. Earth Angels have parental guilt toward everything that needs caretaking on this planet, including people, animals, plants, bodies of water, and so forth.

- You believe that you're loved for what you do, instead of who you are. So, unless you're doing "enough" or the "right thing," you feel undeserving of love.

When you were in the spirit world as a celestial angel, you could help on a very wide scale. Yet, you were still limited in the aid you could offer because people have freewill choices. Not even God can intervene when someone has made a freewill choice to suffer, or perform a hurtful deed.

Now that you're in a physical body, you're even more restricted as to how many people you can affect at once. Physical bodies give you certain limitations that you didn't have when you were a celestial angel. This can create a low-level feeling of frustration, because deep down you remember being able to travel wherever you were needed instantly. You remember being able to defy physical laws and enact miraculous solutions. And while you still have access to all of your spiritual gifts, the dense physical plane slows everything down.

As a result of all these factors, you feel guilty—when it's not your fault! By taking on a physical body, you've traded in one set of superpowers for another set. For example, people generally don't listen to their guardian angels. They either don't hear the voice of their angels, or they don't trust or believe the messages that they receive.

So you took on a human body because people *do* listen to other people. You're still a messenger for God, except now as a human you can be louder and easier to understand.

So we Earth Angels need to let go of guilt about not having easy access to our celestial spiritual gifts.

◦—◦

Some guilt occurs when you do something that you believe is wrong. For instance, if you believe that cigarette smoking is harmful and low-vibrational, and you still smoke, you're betraying yourself and the result will be guilt. Same thing if you believe it's wrong to eat junk food, get drunk, have an affair, cheat on an exam . . . and yet you do these things anyway. As long as you're engaged in behaviors you feel bad about, guilt will be the natural consequence.

Guilt is a very low-vibrational energy. The angels say that guilt clips the wings of lightworkers. It makes us less effective as healers and manifestors.

So, if you're engaging in behaviors you don't feel good about, there are two ways to handle this:

1. **Stop doing the behavior!** This is likely the healthiest route to take. Admittedly, it's not the easiest path, but that's why following this option makes you stronger and raises your self-esteem.

2. **Change what you believe about the behavior!** Guilt is more toxic than any behavior you can engage in. So if you're going to continue with it, it's essential that you let go of the guilt surrounding it. Meditate, pray, do research, talk to trusted people, and take other healthy steps to realign your beliefs about the behavior so that you truly can engage in it guilt-free.

Everyone Has Free Will

As we've discussed, a lot of guilt occurs because other people are unhappy and we blame ourselves for being unable to fix them. This is where we have to remember "freewill choices." We naturally assume that everyone wants to be happy. This is because we know that happiness is the highest vibration, and one that's healing and healthy. So why wouldn't everyone want to be happy?

In spiritual truth, we were all created equally happy, because we were made in the image and likeness of God, Who's pure bliss, joy, and happiness. So deep down, we already *are* happy in our souls!

But in this 3-D physical world of duality and polarities, there are opposing forces to everything. So the opposite of happiness would be depression. Some people's lives are dedicated to experiencing duality opposites, and they go to dark extremes in order to push their ability to feel. There are some people who don't feel alive unless they feel depressed. And one could argue that you're in that category, too! After all, if you're not allowing yourself to be happy, just because someone else is unhappy, aren't *you* also contributing to unhappiness in the world?

Wanting everyone to be happy ultimately is very controlling. You're making the decision for others what emotional state they should be in. And then you might be pressuring them to follow your advice so that they can feel happy. That's really rude and, ultimately, borders on playing God.

Everyone makes their own choices, and while you can be a very positive influence and role model for others, in the end it's up to them to choose whether to be happy or not. Love means respecting someone's choices for themselves.

Of course, if a loved one goes into clinical depression, you'd definitely want to intervene and seek professional help. Depression can lead to serious health consequences and even suicide.

But for an average amount of sadness, give people space to make up their own minds if that's how they want to live. This will make your life a whole lot easier. You don't have to be in charge anymore, which is a very freeing realization! And if you don't enjoy being with someone who chooses to be chronically unhappy, know that you don't have to spend time with him or her!

Worry

Worry arises when you try to control the future by figuring out what bad things might happen so that you can prevent them.

The trouble with worry as a control device is that the opposite of what you desire always occurs. What you worry about tends to happen. It's an extremely low-vibrational energy that causes tension in your face, body, and mind.

Worry pushes away other people, who are consciously or unconsciously repelled by the low energy of this emotion. So, worrying can leave you feeling lonely and afraid at a time when you need support. In addition, by obsessively worrying about something, you'll tend to manifest that very thing in a self-fulfilling prophecy.

So instead of helping you control the future, worry actually brings about everything you *don't* want. It's probably one of the worst defense mechanisms that you can adopt.

Worry can be an inherited habit. If you saw your parents worrying a lot, you may have adopted this behavior as a normal part of life. Sometimes parents feel that this is a requirement of love. Some parents even tell their children: "I only worry about you because I love you." And then the child grows up confusing worry with love.

Of course it's normal to be worried about our children! But when we realize that this emotion helps nothing and can often bring about negative results, we become more motivated to turn this around.

Worry can become an addictive habit as well. (Addictions are obsessive and compulsive behaviors that create temporary relief and happiness, followed by long-term pain.) Worry can briefly give you the feeling that you'll be able to master and control the situation, so it becomes your go-to coping habit. In addition to the behavioral addiction to this emotion, excessive worry can also lead to substance addictions that you turn to in an attempt to calm yourself down.

People who worry a great deal have a sense of doom-and-gloom about their future. They expect the worst, often as a way of avoiding being surprised or disappointed if the worst in fact occurs. These are often people who have had challenging and harsh lives, and all they've known is pain and betrayal in their relationships. So it's no wonder that they worry that more pain will come their way.

Chronic worry can suppress your immune system, and you might also experience symptoms of panic attacks and muscular tension. Medical studies show that chronic worriers are more prone to cardiovascular disease and other illness.

—᠅—᠅—

The first thing to know is that you can make a better future for yourself without having to resort to worry. So before you start worrying about worrying, let's talk about some real options for you:

1. Avoid stimulants in food and beverages. Coffee, tea, colas, chocolate, sugar, and other stimulants can make your body nervous and tense, and your mind will attribute this tension to anxiety.

2. Exercise. Blowing off steam through cardiovascular exercise such as jogging, running, using an elliptical trainer, yoga, fast walking, swimming, bicycling, dancing, and so forth is a wonderful way to reduce or eliminate the worry habit.

3. Turn worries into prayers. Worries never help anything, but prayers always help everything. The next time you're fretting about something, frame your concern into a complete sentence. Either write the worry down on paper, type it on your computer, or say the complete sentence out loud. By facing your worries, you defuse their power over you. Worries, left inside and unconscious, are what create the low-level rumblings of anxiety in the background of your mind and emotions. Next, put the words *God, please help me with this . . .* in front of the worry. You have now turned your worry into a prayer.

As you know, God and the angels can only help you if you give them permission. They respect your freewill choices, and will only intervene if you ask. So by turning worries into prayers, you have just allowed heaven to support you with miraculous solutions.

Dark Night of the Soul

The dark night of the soul occurs when you confront your innermost fears and feel them completely and deeply. For most people, this means facing issues of life and death, the meaning of your life, and whether life is worth living. The dark night of the soul is similar to the initiations that ancient Egyptian candidates for high priest- and priesureshood would endure.

In that culture, you'd be enclosed in a sarcophagus, which is like a coffin, for several days. In that enclosed environment, with no light and just enough air for you not to suffocate, your mind would terrify you as your fears came alive as very realistic hallucinations.

At the end of two or three days, when the sarcophagus was opened up, if you were still alive, you passed the initiation. Some people actually died from fear, even though it was just in their minds. This shows how terrifying our thoughts can be if we were to really confront them head-on.

In a dark night of the soul, you feel totally alone in the world, completely misunderstood, as if you don't fit in anywhere. You feel like your life doesn't matter, so what's the use of carrying on?

Like the ancient Egyptian initiation, the dark night of the soul puts you in a position of life or death. Some people don't survive, because they decide life isn't worth living, and they tragically take their own lives. For some, this suicide takes a slower pace, with the person using toxic addictions to gradually kill themselves.

But if you can stay with the emotions, including the very painful ones, the dark night of the soul can actually lift your whole life to a higher and clearer level.

Nobody wishes for a dark night of the soul, and it's not something that you can create artificially. Basically, it just happens when you least expect it, usually because something has triggered a deep and dark emotional place inside of you.

Dark nights of the soul, like every part of life, serve a healing and useful function. The dark night of the soul is a mirror that you hold up to yourself so that you can see the contents of your ego's fears. A lot of the painful emotions you're experiencing are connected to situations that happened in your childhood. Present-day situations are triggering painful memories.

Don't numb your pain or run away from your emotions. They're your teachers! Just keep asking your painful feelings, *What are you here to teach me?*

Ultimately, it will boil down to this: forgiving yourself and everyone who has ever hurt you is the only way to escape the pain. You don't need to forgive their actions. You definitely *should* still stand up for yourself and be truthful about your feelings. And you don't want to stand for any form of abuse. But forgiveness is essential as the ultimate detox. Let go of the past in all directions of time and finally be free!

CHAPTER SEVEN

BE YOUR OWN
AUTHORITY
FIGURE

*O*ne of the top questions I'm asked is whether someone's dream will be successful or not. Usually people will tell me that they have a dream career, and they wonder whether it's safe to make the change from their current job and move forward in the direction they desire.

As an example, people will often ask me if they're a healer. What they really mean by that question is: "Could I be successful as a professional healer?" They know they're a healer because they've had many experiences where their healing energy has helped someone. But what they don't know for certain is whether they could make it a full-time occupation.

When someone asks me this question, of course I can give him or her a reading. I can see the energy around everyone and how it relates to their ideal career and life purpose. This is something I've been doing with my friends since I was a kid.

While I'm certainly happy to do career and life-purpose readings, what I'd prefer is for people to become their own authority figures. Because what troubles me during these readings is the feeling that the person is giving his or her power away to me. So I always do my best to empower him or her.

We're raised to be *dis*empowered, unfortunately. In school, we're taught that we must raise our hands in order to go to the bathroom, which is a basic and necessary bodily function. We're taught that we have to raise our hands before we can speak, when speaking is another natural function.

Yes, these rules create social parameters and order. But the unfortunate result is that we learn to squelch our natural impulses and instincts. We become overly compliant.

We also learn to rely upon other people giving us permission to do what we want or need to do. This sets up a very unhealthy chain of events. And it leads to people second-guessing themselves as adults.

So if a very talented healer comes to me and she isn't doing healing work because she's second-guessing herself, I consider this a tragedy. Think about how many lives she could have touched and healed if she'd just followed her inner guidance when it first arose.

Stop Playing Life Safe!

Every successful person has to take risks in order for his or her dreams to come true. These risks are both physical and emotional.

A retailer has to risk money by opening up a new store. An author has to risk rejection and loss of time, with many hours spent writing and submitting material to publishers. An artist risks humiliation if others don't appreciate his or her artwork. And activists risk being labeled as conspiracy theorists, negative, or paranoid because they're speaking out about social issues.

Playing it safe in life gets you nowhere. Playing by the rules doesn't give you an *A+* in life. There's no one in the sky with a clipboard judging each of your actions.

Yes, there are actions that can bring more love to the world or more pain. And as Earth Angels, we have missions to bring more love into the world and to avoid bringing pain to others.

When people ask me whether their dream career would be successful, what they really mean is: "Can I pay my bills doing what I love?" And here's the truthful answer, based upon my many decades of studying what makes someone successful in terms of worldly success and emotional success (that is, happiness):

The truth about any dream is that virtually everything is accessible and attainable for everyone. There really are no blocks. Ninety-nine percent of blocks that you experience are coming from your own fears. And those fears are projections that you place onto your path by worrying about the future.

When we worry: *Could this happen?* or *Could that happen?* we are planting the seeds of those feared situations coming to pass. We always meet our future worries upon the path.

The Secret to Success

Anything that you dream of and are willing to work toward will succeed. Anything that you're willing to take risks for will go well.

The most successful people work for themselves. They rarely hold jobs working for someone else. So if you want to significantly increase your satisfaction levels with your job, as well as your income, you must be your own boss. It's wise to begin your self-employment part-time and keep your regular job to pay the bills. As your self-employment gradually becomes more successful and your income increases, you can eventually quit your day job. But this doesn't happen magically on its own. You have to take the risk of starting your self-employment. You have to assume financial and emotional risks to do so, but the rewards are enormously worth it.

God is your employer. You might say that we Earth Angels work for God Inc. And just like any ethical, good company, all employees of God Inc. are given plenty of support and are well supplied.

All you have to do to get ahead and have wonderful assignments, as well as raises and promotions, is follow the guidance that you receive as an employee of God Inc.

Have you ever worked for a company where there's an employee who argues with every assignment he or she is given? Does this employee tend to get recognition or raises?

Usually not!

The employees who tend to get promotions and raises are those who have the team spirit and who follow the directives they're given from management.

So it is with God Inc.: you're given assignments, and they may seem to have nothing to do with your career objectives.

For example, you may get a strong inner urge to quit drinking alcohol or change to a primarily vegetarian diet. You might be called upon to move to a new city, to let go of certain toxic relationships, or to begin a yoga practice.

These are examples of common assignments from God Inc. These assignments might not seem to make any sense. You might think they have nothing to do with your responsibilities. But quite simply, if you do your assignments, you'll get wonderful rewards. If you delay, hesitate, or argue about the assignments you're given, don't expect to get very far. You'll still be loved and honored for who you are, but won't be given the cool assignments that would speak to your soul.

Lightwork

Earth Angels are sometimes called *lightworkers,* and the two terms are fairly interchangeable. I bring this up because I want to point out that the term is light*worker,* not light*rester.*

As Earth Angels, we're here to work! You and I have big jobs to do. Most likely, you can feel the depth and largeness of your life purpose energetically within you. It might feel like an inner pressure to help the world. It might be a sense of God's alarm clock ringing inside of you, pushing you to get up and go make a positive difference.

Being your own authority figure means that you trust this inner guidance and you follow it without hesitation or delay.

So the balance of all of this is:

1. You need to be very aware of your true feelings, physically and emotionally.

2. It's important to expend daily effort on your dream. It doesn't even matter *what* you do related to your dream, as long as there's some action every day.

This shows a teamwork approach with heaven. You always have freewill choices, so ultimately you're in control and in charge of your own destiny. However, if you're praying for some happy outcome, you'll need to team up with God and the heavenly angels.

So it's a matter of teamwork and not about being independent or dependent.

You get an inner intuitive nudging to take some sort of action step. Perhaps the inner nudge is to make a healthy life change or to do something constructive.

That inner intuitive knowledge is your assignment from God Inc. The question then becomes: *Will you enact that assignment and follow the directives given?*

You have free will, so you don't have to do anything. There are a million reasons why people don't follow their Divine assignments. They may argue passionately why they can't do what they're asked to do. Their arguments may cite that they don't have enough time, money, or information; or they lack a sense of readiness and aren't prepared or confident enough. The list of reasons why they can't fulfill their Divine assignments goes on and on.

But what if those employees of God Inc. instead put that same amount of passion into taking the risk to try one action step in the direction of fulfilling their assignment?

The answer is that when you take one action step in the direction of your inner guidance, the universe matches you with an equal amount of support and wonderful new opportunities.

Your greatest dreams almost always match your life purpose. God Inc. wants you to be happy, healthy, abundantly supplied, intellectually stimulated, and emotionally and spiritually fulfilled. God Inc. doesn't want unhappy employees!

But God Inc. does want one thing: employees who will say yes to their assignments without arguing, without delaying, and without trying to change them to match their egos' will.

Will You Be a "Yes-Woman" or "Yes-Man" for God?

If you say yes to God's Divine assignments, you'll be handsomely rewarded with wonderful challenges, fun opportunities, and plenty of promotions and raises.

So the bottom line of all of this is: any dream that you're willing to put the effort and work into will come about!

But you must be willing to do the action steps. Every successful person really does work hard. Every Earth Angel is here to do work.

As a healer, for example, you'll need to take some of the following action steps:

- Keep your mind and body detoxified and clear so that you can channel the highest-vibrational energies through you.

- Take classes or read books about different healing modalities.

- Practice doing healing work on yourself, your loved ones, your pets, or plants.

- Market yourself by having a website or social-media page devoted to your healing practice. (You could have a partner such as a spouse or a close friend function as a manager for your practice.)

Or if you dream of becoming a published author, the action steps to take include:

- Make an outline of what topic you want to explore with your writing.

- Sit down on a regular basis and do the writing.

- Be willing to submit what you've written to publishers, without letting any rejection stop you from pursuing your dream.

A process that has worked for me includes making deadlines with myself. When I first started to write, I was extremely busy with my two young sons, a full-time career as an insurance secretary, and my part-time studies at the local college. It would have been very easy for me to rationalize away my dream of being a published author by saying that I was much too busy. Because that was very true: I *was* busy!

It's easy to get overwhelmed with the enormity of a dream. This is especially true if you don't know exactly how you're going to get to the finish line. And the truth is that any dream that has come true always manifests in unexpected and highly creative ways.

So you really can't foresee all of the twists and turns that moving forward with your dream is going to take you on. And there are no guarantees that you'll have a completely smooth path. In fact, I can guarantee that there will be moments of disappointment along the way. But don't let that stop you!

Your dream is your baby, and the fact that you have the thought of it inside of you is a form of gestation. Your dream needs you to carry it to term by taking daily action steps to nurture, support, and grow it into full realization.

If you make a habit of taking daily action steps, you'll find your path much more quickly and more clearly than by simply dreaming about it.

Every day, do some action step related to your dream—it doesn't matter what. The action steps stimulate your creativity and your awareness of opportunities.

Sometimes people are afraid to move forward with their dreams because of the fear of success or failure. It's easier to just hold the dream inside instead of finding out that it may never come true. But that stagnation is deadening to your energy.

Always remember that your dreams *will* ultimately help others. By fulfilling *yours,* you'll inspire others to do the same themselves. And your dream of being a healer, teacher, artist, or writer will directly benefit those whose lives you touch.

So if you're unwilling to take action steps to help yourself with your dream, do it for those you care about!

What issue in this world really pushes your buttons? What are you passionate about or upset about? On what topic do you frequently think, *Someone should do something about this!*

Well, that someone's you!

Make a promise to yourself that every day you'll take one action step related to your dream, such as:

- Reading new research
- Practicing
- Writing
- Reaching out to those who are experts
- Doing marketing efforts
- Creating visualization tools

Visualization tools include clipping pictures from magazines, as well as writing or cutting out inspirational phrases that are all related to your dreams coming true. Glue those pictures and words on a large poster-board backing. And then place that vision board somewhere where you'll see it daily.

Each time you look at the vision board, say silently: *Thank You, God, for these dreams being true right now.*

It's very important that you envision your dreams already being true in the present moment. If you think of them as always being something that will happen at a later date, you'll keep them perpetually away from you, suspended in the future.

Even if you don't feel prepared yet, even if you don't feel completely clear about what it is you're doing or

where you're going, do *something.* Even if you're convinced that you're the world's busiest person, take action
steps related to your dream every day.

PART II

DEVELOPING ASSERTIVENESS *in* RELATIONSHIPS

CHAPTER EIGHT

EARTH ANGELS
AND
RELATIONSHIPS

A healthy relationship is one in which each person is free to be honest with the other, in loving ways. In a healthy relationship, each person's needs are respected. Conflicts will arise, as they do anytime two or more people are together, but in a healthy relationship, they will be cleared through honest and loving discussions.

As we've talked about throughout this book, the foundation of assertiveness is your willingness to be honest with yourself and others. This requires you to be in touch with your feelings and opinions. So you'll need to ground yourself and be conscious of your physical *and* emotional feelings. Both forms of feelings are honest messages that are direct pipelines to heaven.

Getting Grounded

Earth Angels float above their physical selves like a helium balloon on a string. They're blissfully unaware of how their bodies feel or how their emotions are doing, because they're up in the ethers with God and the celestial angels.

While it feels great to have your head in the clouds, this could be a distraction from your earthly life purpose. You're in a human physical body for a reason, and it's important that Earth Angels learn how to put their focus and consciousness into their bodies.

You can ground yourself by spending time outdoors in nature, especially by going barefoot and touching the soil, sand, or grass. You can also do so by simply surrounding yourself with trees and plants.

Eating vegetables can help you get grounded, including potatoes, radishes, turnips, onions, and other bulb vegetables. They grow in the ground, so they ground *you* when you eat them. Just make sure that they're organic and non–genetically modified (GMO-free).

You can also ground your awareness by touching your feet or even better, getting a foot rub, pedicure, or session of reflexology.

Honestly Revealing Your Feelings

Once your consciousness is back in your body, you'll have an easier time of being in touch with what you really feel emotionally and physically.

This allows you to pay attention to your reactions around different people. You'll notice when, for example, your stomach muscles tighten in the presence of a certain person.

You'll notice when your heart rate accelerates with anxiety around someone else. You'll be aware when you feel resentful, shamed, or angry, especially when the individual in question exhibits a specific type of behavior.

A passive person holds his or her feelings inside and never reveals them to others, for fear of offending them or pushing them away. In this type of relationship, the passive person is extremely lonely because no one truly knows him or her. The only cure is to be vulnerable and honest with others so that they can love you for who you really are instead of who you project yourself to be with a false persona.

Our honesty with other people isn't designed to manipulate or change them. That would constitute being aggressive or passive-aggressive. We share our honest feelings because that's what healthy relationship partners do. Instead of worrying about the other person's reactions, take that time and energy to gather your thoughts and think of ways to be honest that are gentle and supportive.

As an Earth Angel, you're naturally loving and kind. Being honest is a part of that loving and kind nature. It shows that you care enough about the person in the relationship to keep it long-lasting and healthy.

In business relationships, being honest earns you respect. Honest people are viewed as strong contenders for advancement in the business world. Your genuineness is a sign that you have substance and strength, which is what healthy organizations seek in their employees. And you'll be much happier working for a healthy organization!

As we previously discussed, those who are "phony nice" are instantly spotted as weaklings whom shark-like people take advantage of. "Phony nice" means having an insincere smile and agreeing to things that most people would never agree to. Everyone can spot a person who's being real, as well as identify someone who's pretending to be happy when he or she is obviously not. "Phony nice" also means that you defer to others' opinions and never formulate or stand up for your own ideas. "Phony nice" people rarely get raises or promotions at work. Those who are real are admired and promoted, because they're trustworthy. People sing their praises: "She's so real!"

While you're being honest, it's important to own your feelings, as we previously discussed. That means avoiding pointing fingers, and not using blaming words or a sharp tone of voice.

It's about being honest from a place of love. This is the highest vibration of communication, similar to how the angels are truthful with you, even telling you things and guiding you in ways that are uncomfortable for you to hear, such as when they urge you to improve your diet or lifestyle.

Honesty is part of being a good and loving friend. It's important to be gentle yet firm while being honest. What this means is that your tone of voice is melodic and sweet, without tension in your throat or inflection. But at the same time, you're clear and steady, such as looking the other person in the eye directly.

Come across as friendly, but also be sincere. If you're angry, it's okay to show it. You're human, with human emotions. When you're real, other people trust you more because they can tell that your words match your energy.

Most Earth Angels are terrified of their own anger. They're afraid that they'll lose control if they finally unleash their hidden anger. But actually, releasing it a bit at a time is similar to letting the air out of the balloon slowly. You have more control when you don't have pent-up anger inside of you.

Be honest with the other person, without trying to control or manipulate him or her to react in a certain way. Tell it like it is and let the chips fall where they may. If people react with anger, those are *their* feelings, and they have a right to their feelings. Now, what they do with their anger is a whole different story. You never have to take others' abusive words or behavior! It doesn't matter what your relationship is, or how much you need them in your life. If they're yelling at you, name-calling, or threatening you in any way, walk away.

Red Flags

The angels will always protect you from entering toxic relationships, *provided that you pay attention to the signs they send to you.* If you don't listen, you'll end up in a toxic or even abusive relationship. In relationships, these signs are called *red flags,* which are cautionary messages you receive from your intuition, your body's signals, and your angels.

When you meet someone new, your stomach will tell you immediately about the energy of the person and of the potential relationship. Always pay attention to what your stomach does in the presence of another person, because it will tell you the truth. That's why they say to *trust your gut*.

If your stomach muscles tighten, it's a sign that you're stressed in that person's presence. It can also mean that the other person is stressed around you, and you're picking up on his or her tension. Either way, you're feeling tension, and that's something to consider when deciding whether or not to move forward with this relationship.

Next, watch the person's actions and listen to his or her words. Notice any signs that he or she is lying to others and bragging about how he or she got away with something, or any other exhibition of unethical tendencies. Watch for any talk of racism or racist jokes. Also, notice if the person gossips about mutual friends or puts people down in unkind ways. Yes, it might be amusing to engage in gossip about others or laugh at them behind their backs. But know that this person will also be trash-talking and gossiping about *you*.

Every time your stomach gets tense, that's one red flag. With each new person, you'll want to be conscious of these red flags before you completely open yourself up to him or her. If you get red-flag warnings about someone's character, that's your angels' way of protecting you. The angels are trying to steer you away from that relationship.

Standing Your Ground

Sometimes you might be saying things to people that they don't want to hear. And you, as an intuitive Earth Angel, *know* that this isn't what they want to hear. You may react to that person's anger or disappointment as you're honest with them. You may even consider backing down from your opinion. This is where practice is needed to develop the inner strength to stand your ground.

Of course, as an Earth Angel, you'll listen to others' opinions, too. You'll give them the respect that you want for yourself, but watch out for the trap that sensitive people sometimes fall into where they silence their opinions and feelings because the other person gets louder.

Don't cave in just because someone gets loud or in-your-face with their opinions. Don't engage in a power struggle, either. Very often, power struggles arise because of one person's need for attention and validation. You can defuse a power struggle by making your own power so large that the other person feels it unconsciously, and backs down. You can enlarge your energy by breathing deeply, and on each inhalation feel yourself drawing power up from the core of the earth, through the bottoms of your feet and up into your body. Visualize your energy and power being enormously large, and the other person will back down.

People don't change much, and you certainly can't be the one to change them. There's an old saying: "A leopard doesn't change its spots." What this means is that people basically continue to have the same sort of behavior patterns and personalities throughout their lives. And yet Earth Angels are constantly disappointed and surprised by this very basic human concept.

I've run into this myself. For instance, a person will ask me to give a workshop at a conference, and I notice right off the bat that the producer is very disorganized and doesn't follow through with e-mails or other forms of communication. But I rationalize that this is just a temporary behavior from this person. And that's because I'm projecting my ideals of how I believe others "should" act. Then as the event gets closer in time and the producer continues to be disorganized, I shouldn't be surprised, because this is how he or she had been with me originally.

Defining Your Own Self

Don't allow others to define you. Another person's opinion about you is just that: an opinion. It doesn't matter how often someone states it, or how loudly. It's still an opinion and not fact.

If disparaging or mean things are being said to you, that's a form of abuse. No one has the right to call you names, tell you what you can or can't do, or make you feel bad about yourself. There are some people who are incapable of giving approval or the amount of love that an Earth Angel needs and deserves. Pray for that person, but don't waste your valuable earthly time hanging out with him or her.

><

CHAPTER NINE

TOXIC RELATIONSHIPS:

HOW TO RECOGNIZE AND HANDLE THEM

*E*arth Angels are "nice" people, with big, open hearts, so they can't see when they're involved in toxic relationships. They excuse and minimize other people's behavior: "He didn't mean to act that way. He was having a bad day."

Even more toxic is when Earth Angels blame themselves for someone's harsh behavior: "If I were nicer [or thinner, smarter, richer, etc.], then he'd treat me better." This is nonsense! Don't take responsibility for someone's cruel treatment.

Earth Angels tolerate harsh and even abusive relationships because they're afraid of being alone, being in the wrong, or being judged. They force themselves to rise above mistreatment by disconnecting from their feelings.

Dissociation from your feelings does no one any good. It makes you out of touch with your physical body, which can lead you to overeat without realizing you're full. It can also lead you to ignore symptoms that need immediate healing treatment.

Dissociation also keeps you from sensing your emotions. When you're numb, you can't hear your angels' messages. Your sensitivity shuts down. Since heaven's messages come on the frequency of your attunement to energy, you need to be in touch with your feelings.

Earth Angels don't know any better than to stay in a harsh relationship, because they haven't had a lot of experience with human relationships. After all, they're used to living in the higher-vibrational realms! This has led them to be socially awkward, and they may feel terribly lonely. So they allow *any* relationship to persist because they don't want to be alone.

As an Earth Angel, you're a teacher for peace. If you take the harsh treatment others dish out, how will they learn? Also, if someone's treating *you* harshly, he or she is definitely doing the same to others. By your teaching him or her a better way to behave, you can prevent other people from being mistreated.

Harsh and Toxic Behavior

When you first meet people, they're on their best behavior. They'll agree with you, even if they really don't. It can take up to two years before you see the real person. That's why it's important for Earth Angels to take things slowly in their romantic relationships and friendships. Until you get to know the real person, don't get married to—or go into a long-term business with—him or her.

In any relationship, there's a synergy (energy exchange) between both people. Unless you're being authentic, you don't know how well you interact. If you're both pretending when it comes to your feelings and opinions, and being falsely polite and insincere, there's no real relationship.

The following pages list the most common types of toxic relationship behaviors for you to recognize, and how to deal with them in honest and assertive ways that are healthful for you and the other person. These examples give you guidance as to how to assertively handle toxic situations.

Most Earth Angels have been beaten up by life and suffer from low self-esteem and feelings of worthlessness. So they often don't recognize abusive and toxic patterns in their relationships. Earth Angels don't know any better than to accept hurtful behavior from others. They deny and excuse such behavior, while secretly suffering in silence. So this list will help you not feel ashamed or alone in your relationship patterns, and also give you a way out.

By pointing out these harsh relationship patterns, we're not judging the individuals involved. Many times, Earth Angels are so wary of being judgmental that they overdo acceptance. This isn't about judging another person; it's about being aware of the dynamics within the relationship.

Sometimes, style differences between you and the other person are what cause the harsh energy of the relationship. For example: You're quiet and gentle, and he's loud and rough. You're spontaneous and go with the flow, but she's all about planning and organizing. Through awareness and honesty, style differences can be negotiated harmoniously if each person is willing to compromise and have compassion for the other person's style. However, where abuse is involved, the relationship needs to end and healing needs to begin.

This list is to open your eyes and help you to be aware of your honest feelings when you're with other people. It also gives you some suggestions for assertive ways to manage these various scenarios. There's no implication that you need to leave or abandon anyone; however, you *do* need to take care of yourself and any children affected by your being in a toxic relationship.

Interrupting

The person who continually interrupts you doesn't really care what you have to say. Interrupters are people who are anxious to hear the sound of their own voice, and who are convinced that they provide the most interesting and accurate conversation. Very often, the interrupter is someone who's abusing caffeine or other stimulants, making him or her anxious and hyperactive.

— **How this relationship affects you:** If you're in a relationship with an interrupter, you begin to talk really fast to get your words in before they can be interrupted. You start to feel anxious whenever the interrupter initiates conversation with you.

— **How to handle this:** Assertive Earth Angels will stop someone the first time he or she interrupts them and say "Excuse me, I wasn't finished talking" in a very calm and peaceful way. If you touch the person's arm while saying this sentence, the impact is even stronger. Remember that you're helping the other person become aware of a habit that's likely blocking him or her in all other relationships, personal and professional. You're teaching how to be a better communicator.

Correcting

Correcting is similar to interrupting, except worse. People who are prone to this behavior not only interrupt you, but also "correct" what you've been saying. They may point out errors in your grammar or pronunciation, like your old English teacher. Or they may tell you much more about the topic you're discussing.

While it's great to learn new facts and proper grammar, it's this person's *continual* correcting that becomes tiring. No one likes to feel small or stupid, and that's how you feel when you're with this person. You always feel "one-down" from him or her. Some people engage in correcting behavior because that's how they show that they care about and love you. They believe that by "improving" you, they're helping you. Other times, correctors conduct this behavior out of an unconscious habit.

— **How this relationship affects you:** Anxiety around a corrector is a normal response. You walk on eggshells, worried about the next mistake you'll make. If you live with one, it will affect your self-esteem. You may doubt your own intelligence, and give your power away to the other person, because you believe that you can't do anything right.

— **How to handle this:** As an assertive Earth Angel, you must face these situations head-on, so you'll need to tell the corrector how you honestly feel. By giving candid feedback to the corrector, you help him or her develop better relationships. If his or her correcting style annoys you, it annoys everyone else, too. So, the next time this person corrects you, take a deep breath and say: "Sometimes I feel that you're more my teacher than my friend. And while I appreciate you adding to my body of knowledge, I'd prefer to have conversations where it's just us sharing our feelings instead of you trying to teach me."

One-upmanship

People who one-up others have done everything better than you, on a larger scale, and they want to tell you about it! Any story that you relate will be scarcely digested before it is regurgitated in a more grandiose version—starring *them*. Such people only listen enough to hear the topic of discussion so that they can immediately go to their memory banks and extract their experience of that situation, which was over-the-top amazing. They're so insecure and desperate for attention and approval that they step all over other people's spotlight to grab it back for themselves.

— **How this relationship affects you:** Your body exhibits signs of tension and resentment. You feel unheard and unappreciated. In this sort of relationship, you feel lonely because it's a one-sided conversation at all times. You also feel disappointed that the other person won't share in your excitement or other emotions concerning the experiences you're relaying.

— **How to handle this**: Such people have no idea that they're upsetting, annoying, or pushing others away with their superiority complex. They're extremely lonely and wonder why people aren't impressed with their accomplishments. They believe that if people are impressed, they'll be loved and valued. Once you understand the depth of such a person's loneliness and desperation to be loved, an assertive Earth Angel can go from there.

The heart of assertiveness is being honest and taking responsibility for your feelings. So never point the finger and claim that the other person is making you angry. It's his or her *behavior* that's triggering you. Let the one-upper know that you value and admire him or her, as long as that's sincerely how you feel. You don't offer these compliments unless you really believe them, or else you're manipulating and trying to control the other person's reaction to you, which is dysfunctional and dishonest. Explain that you'd love to share your own experience and enjoy the details, without turning the tables to talk about his or her experience right away. Tell the person that sharing experiences is like enjoying a really good meal, and you want to savor each course one at a time.

Clingy Neediness

Clingy people are insecure individuals who latch onto whoever will acknowledge their existence by giving them attention. As a caring Earth Angel, you can sense that such people need love. The problem is that they're a bottomless pit of neediness, which neither you nor anyone else can fill. This person is constantly texting, calling, and e-mailing you. He or she may even pop over unannounced for visits. This individual may have a misconceived notion of the degree of your friendship, and mistakenly believe that you're best friends when you're actually casual acquaintances.

— **How this relationship affects you:** This person has you looking over your shoulder constantly in an effort to avoid him or her. You start to feel guilty because you know that this person enjoys your company and feels he or she needs you, even though in a spiritual sense no one needs anyone as their Source.

— **How to handle this:** It's important for you, as an assertive Earth Angel, to always tell the truth with love. So you'll need to summon the courage to tell this person that you're quite busy with projects and need more space. This insecure person will likely feel wounded and take your words personally, but you can't put your whole life on hold to coddle someone. You're enabling unhealthy behavior by pretending to be friends. Perhaps there's someone else who would genuinely enjoy this person's company, and if you get out of the way by being honest, it leaves room for that new and more appropriate individual to come into his or her life.

Stalking

Stalkers take the needy and clingy behavior to a whole new, and sometimes dangerous, level. Almost always, this is an ex-lover who won't let go. He or she shows up at work, your home, or your friends' homes; calls you constantly; and incessantly begs you to return to the relationship. Very often, these pleas are accompanied by promises that he or she has "really" changed this time. If you don't comply with the person's wishes, the behavior may escalate to abuse or threats.

— **How this relationship affects you:** For some people, having a stalker is a misguided boost to their self-esteem. But make no mistake, stalkers don't love you. They want to own and control you, which is the opposite of true love. If the stalker is telling you that his or her life is ruined without you, or threatening to commit suicide if you don't come back, you may be racked with guilt and worry. This person has probably caused you great anxiety and even sleepless nights. In extreme cases, you may have had to file for a restraining order to keep him or her away from you.

— **How to handle this:** Don't give this person the satisfaction of any form of reaction. Any reply that you offer encourages him or her to continue stalking you. Have the stalker's number blocked from your phone, or change yours if you have to. Block him or her on your e-mail and social-media sites. Have no contact with the person whatsoever. If there's any history of violence, contact authorities and file for a restraining order. Don't take threats lightly. Stalkers have committed violent crimes many times. Call upon Archangel Michael to cast this person permanently out of your life, and vow that in any future relationships where there are signs of extreme jealousy, controlling behaviors, or stalking, you'll run the other way.

Guilt-Tripping

Guilt-trippers are practically professionals at getting their way through manipulating other people. They won't take no for an answer. They have a well-rehearsed bag of tricks they use to cajole others and get what they want. They might cry, threaten to hurt themselves, say that no one loves them, or remind you of the times that they helped you.

— **How this relationship affects you:** You feel resentful or even enraged that you're being pushed against your will, but you feel you have no choice but to comply with the guilt-tripper's wishes. If you feel yourself being pushed to help someone through guilt or implied obligation, this is a sign that you're being manipulated.

— **How to handle this:** By facing this situation directly, you will accelerate your spiritual growth. Guilt-trippers aren't accustomed to hearing "no," but it's good for their spiritual growth to have that experience. After all, they have no close relationships because they don't have authentic one-on-one connections with anyone. All of their relationships are egocentric. So, by telling this person no and sticking to it, without guilt or excuses, you're giving the guilt-tripper the opportunity to have a spiritual-growth experience of his or her own. The guilt-tripper will either find another victim to harass or will realize that these methods aren't healthy or effective. This is especially true if everyone in your circle agrees to stop enabling the behavior, and all of you say no to guilt-based requests.

Angerholism

"Angerholics" are addicted to being angry. They get mad at the smallest and slightest provocation, and must immediately announce that they're angry. Such a person has a short fuse and a hot temper. He or she may inflict emotional, verbal, or even physical pain on others. Angerholics always have a justification for why they're angry, and rarely take responsibility themselves.

— **How this relationship affects you:** As an Earth Angel who greatly dislikes conflict, you're highly sensitive to the energy of anger. You therefore walk on eggshells around angry people. You do everything you can possibly think of to appease them. You may even take the blame for their anger, especially if they're yelling that it's all your fault.

— **How to handle this:** Angerholics usually come from a dysfunctional family, and require professional therapy in order to confront their addiction to anger. For this reason, you and your love alone will not unravel their angry tendencies. These are people who get angry at everything. Release the fantasy that you'll find the winning combination that will finally make them happy and peaceful. Stop bending over backward and twisting yourself into knots in order to please such a person. This is a relationship that you may need to leave or distance yourself from, unless the person commits to intense therapy.

Unreliability

Unreliable people promise to help you, but forget to follow through. They miss appointments with you, are never on time for your get-togethers, and can't be counted on to honor their commitments.

— **How this relationship affects you:** For the Earth Angel with low self-esteem, this relationship leaves you feeling unloved and not valued. You start to think that this is your fault, and that if only you were "better," then this person would be more reliable. For an Earth Angel with high self-esteem, you realize that this is an unreliable person, and it's not your fault. Therefore, this relationship may make you angry and prone to complain about your unreliable friend.

— **How to handle this:** The assertive Earth Angel handles all situations directly. With the unreliable person, you must set firm and clear boundaries. The next time the person makes an appointment with you, explain that your time is valuable and that if he or she is not there within 15 minutes of the appointed time, you'll need to leave. You must set boundaries with the person ahead of time, or you may end up feeling like a victim—which you're not.

Nosiness

Busybodies entertain themselves by putting their noses into everyone else's business. They boost their own insecurities by taking pride in knowing the intimate details of everyone's lives—which they will share as the latest gossip. They may even create drama among people in their circle, just so that they have more entertainment to watch unfold. That particular behavior pattern is known as the *pot-stirrer*. They often use subterfuge and deceitful tactics to get you to admit personal details to them, which they'll then immediately blab about to others.

— **How this relationship affects you:** This type of relationship may confuse you, unless you're in touch with your feelings and trust them. An Earth Angel who's new to this sort of behavior may mistake prying questions as being a sign that someone actually cares.

— **How to handle this:** If you have the feeling that someone doesn't care about you and your life but is just pressing for details to entertain him- or herself as if you're a reality show, *trust that feeling*. Stop feeding the shark! Don't share any further information about your life. When you're asked intimate questions, the direct and honest answer is "I'd rather not discuss this." If you say this enough times to nosy people, they'll move on to another target. Or, in the best-case scenario, they'll wake up and discontinue their dysfunctional and hurtful behavior.

Grumpiness

Grumpy people are frequently in a foul mood, either due to physical pain, because of hangovers from addictions, or because they blame everyone for their unhappiness. In extreme cases, grumpiness can lead to psychological or verbal abuse.

— **How this relationship affects you:** It's never fun to be around a grumpy person, especially if you take it personally and blame yourself. If this individual starts name-calling or attacks you verbally, your self-esteem will be wounded and depression can set in.

— **How to handle this:** No matter what reason a person has for grumpiness, he or she is still not allowed to violate your deal-breaker boundaries. There's never an excuse to abuse someone with unkind words. So, state your boundaries clearly and then make no exceptions. If the person continues to violate them, you must leave or distance yourself. Give any guilt to heaven for healing and transmuting (and read about "Getting Rid of Guilt" in Chapter 6).

Accusatory Tendencies

Accusatory people constantly deflect their own feelings of guilt onto others. They never listen to reason, and they jump to conclusions. They're very unpleasant to be around, because they're always causing drama with their unfounded accusations and blaming.

— **How this relationship affects you:** If you're not attuned to accusers' games, you may play right into their hands. If that's the case, you'll accept their blame and feel guilty and bad about yourself. If you have caught on, though, you'll understand that you're not at fault. And your reaction will be anger, hurt, or confusion. You might engage in blaming wars, where you both hurl accusations at each other in an unending battle.

— **How to handle this:** This person is always looking for a fight, so virtually anything you say will be put into the blender of his or her mind and turned into something that's completely different from what you've said. This person is usually out of touch with reality and only listens to his or her own ego's twisted logic. Therefore, the assertive Earth Angel handles the situation directly but also realizes the futility of argument.

On the one hand, if you don't stand up to accusations, they may grow in size and scope within your family, company, or community. However, you needn't engage in a merry-go-round of defending yourself continuously. Usually, the only way to deal with accusers is to be very firm and even loud as you tell them that they're mistaken in their accusation. Don't hurl counter-accusations or put-downs. Keep the conversation clean, brief, and on-topic. If this is a business situation and you're certain of your innocence, you may need to state that inaccurate accusations are slander that is illegal.

Victimhood/Martyrdom

Martyrs are perpetual victims and complainers. Their view of the world is that it's "them" against "poor-little-me." Probably for their whole lives, they've felt picked on and singled out. They've grown up to believe that they're especially victimized by everyone and every system. Such individuals will tell you, in minute detail, every instance in which they've been taken advantage of. These are usually people with very low energy, bordering on depression. They're not looking for solutions—only acknowledgment and poor-baby sympathy.

— **How this relationship affects you:** It's draining to be around victim-martyrs, because they're constantly talking about the deep dark hole in which they live. At first, you'll be shocked by how much this person has been mistreated throughout his or her life. And you might lose sleep worrying about him or her surviving in this world. But after a while, you catch on that this person has an amazingly long string of bad luck, way beyond statistical chance. You also notice that this person rejects suggestions and advice. He or she will say, "Oh, I've already tried that, and here's why it didn't work."

— **How to handle this:** Since victim-martyrs look for rescuers, and then eventually start to resent their rescuers and persecute them, avoid investing a lot of time in this relationship. There are plenty of true victims who sincerely want help, and who desire to improve their lives. There's no sense in wasting time on someone who only wants to complain. A direct and assertive approach would be to tell this person sincerely that he or she is in your prayers, and that you'll meditate about receiving Divine guidance as to how you can be of assistance. Don't let victim-martyrs tell *you* how you are to help them. Make it clear that you get all of your guidance directly from God. And then stick to this intention. Please don't worry: The victim-martyr is a professional at finding rescuers. If you don't assume that role, another person will come along shortly who will.

Controlling Behavior

Controlling people need to be in charge of everyone and everything. If they aren't in charge, they'll act out immaturely and angrily. They'll pout and they'll shout until everyone bends to their will. They're terribly unpleasant to be around, and they have underlings instead of friends or loved ones.

— **How this relationship affects you:** If this is a relationship that you feel like you can't escape, you'll be perpetually anxious around this person, particularly if it's someone who insists on your doing everything his or her way. These are usually people who have a hidden rulebook, and if you accidentally violate one of their rules, you'll be punished either directly or via passive-aggressive behavior on their part. This could lead to dangerous abuse.

— **How to handle this:** Controlling people usually have deep-seated fears of abandonment, and the only way that they can control their world is by trying to control everyone and everything in their midst. It's unlikely that you alone could help them with their insecurities, without the long-term help of a professional. But since the controlling person thinks that everyone else is the problem, it's unlikely that he or she would agree to the amount of therapy needed. If this is a person you're related to and so will of necessity be in contact with, there's no need to get into a power struggle. There's no point, and it's a no-win. As an assertive person, you have an obligation to your own self-esteem to be honest and direct with everyone about your feelings. Just don't expect to change the other person by doing so. Keep your conversations with the controlling person as brief as possible, and spend your time with more pleasant and easier-to-get-along-with people instead.

Perpetual Clowning

This person jokes instead of listening to you and diverts every serious discussion with humor, and sometimes inappropriate humor.

— **How this relationship affects you:** Perhaps you were initially attracted to this person's sense of humor, but it's gotten old now. Now you view him or her as immature, and incapable of sharing deep and serious discussions.

— **How to handle this:** Everyone has a deep side and real feelings. Perpetual clowns defend themselves against deep-seated painful emotions by staying on the surface of life. Recognize that you have a style difference, and don't try to change this person or yourself. Assertive Earth Angels recognize that not everyone is like them or even compatible with them.

With the perpetual clown, it's best to share your feelings honestly. Touch the person's hand, look him or her in the eyes, and say, "I was hoping that we could have a deeper and more serious side to our relationship, to balance the playful side that I so much enjoy with you." The perpetual clown, who probably got in trouble for goofing off in school, will be pleasantly surprised that someone is taking the time to get to know him or her on a deeper level. This is an example of a toxic relationship that you *can* detox with persistence and a dose of honesty.

Loudness

There will always be those who speak and laugh inordinately loudly. They're the loudest people wherever they go. When you try to have an intimate discussion, these individuals shout all the details for everyone within earshot to hear. They were usually raised in a loud family where they had to fight for attention.

— **How this relationship affects you:** If you're highly sensitive to sounds, this person's voice may be physically and energetically painful to you. If you're in public together, you may feel embarrassed because his or her loud voice and laughter annoy other people. *You,* especially, may become annoyed because you'd like a softer and quieter relationship with this person.

— **How to handle this:** Because loud people don't realize the effect that they're having or believe that it's not that bad, they need a reality check. If you deeply care about such a person and want the relationship to continue, you'll need to tell him or her the truth. Usually someone who's loud has a tough exterior but a delicate interior. So you'll need to be direct enough so the person hears you, but not so blunt that you'd crush his or her insecure core. And sometimes, people who speak loudly have difficultly in hearing, so your honesty may compel them to seek appropriate medical or hearing-aid assistance.

Substance Abuse

This is a person who is addicted to a mood-altering substance such as alcohol; prescription or street drugs, including marijuana; or even socially acceptable chemicals such as those found in sugar, caffeine, nicotine, or chocolate. His or her personality changes as a result of using or not using this substance. He or she may be aggressive or lazy; have mood swings; or be jittery, anxious, or argumentative.

— **How this relationship affects you:** *Codependency* is a term describing the relationship of a person who loves a substance addict. The codependent person blames him- or herself for the addiction, a scenario that is often reinforced by the addict's blaming the codependent person. He or she says, "You made me so mad, and now I have to drink."

Codependent people tend to be anxious, filled with guilt, shame, and remorse. They often turn to their own addictions, particularly food such as sugar or white flour, as a way of stuffing down their own feelings. They want to leave the relationship, but they feel afraid and guilty. If they do leave, they often go right into another addictive relationship until they do deep analysis of their reasons for choosing an addict.

— **How to handle this:** If you have had even one relationship with an addict and you still harbor hurt and pain over this, or if you are currently in a relationship with an addict who is still using and abusing his or her chemical of choice, you need support. The free 12-step groups called Codependents Anonymous and Al-Anon are wonderful forums for getting strength, support, and sanity. You can find Codependents Anonymous or Al-Anon meetings internationally by searching for them on the web, as well as free online virtual meetings.

Lack of Boundaries

A person who doesn't respect any boundaries has no sense of personal space. This individual will often "borrow" your possessions without asking, and then won't take good care of them or won't ever return them to you. He or she will also disrespect your emotional boundaries by offering you unsolicited advice, judgments, and opinions.

— **How this relationship affects you:** You'll feel a lack of control when this person is around, and you'll want to run far away and never see him or her again. If you must have a no-boundaries individual in your life because he or she is your relative or has some other close tie, this type of person can be crazy-making. You'll be frustrated whenever you must spend time with him or her. Such people can be lovable and show you that they really care, but the way in which they do so is disrespectful.

— **How to handle this:** Since this behavior style was probably learned in childhood, it's unlikely that this person is going to change much in adulthood. The best you can do is to be honest and repeat yourself about your parameters and boundaries. For instance, if you live with this person, it's very important to have your own personal space and bedroom. Put a lock and a DO NOT DISTURB sign on your door, and without being passive-aggressive, clearly outline what behavior you will and won't accept. This person usually will hear repeated directness, even if he or she doesn't agree with what's being said.

Name-Calling

Name-callers are verbally abusive, and frequently pepper their conversation with profanities. Sometimes they pretend that they're doing this as a joke and insist that people who get offended don't have a sense of humor. *"I was just kidding!"* they'll say defensively. Other times name-callers hurl these insults and epithets with the energy of anger behind their words.

— **How this relationship affects you:** Name-calling can hurt even more deeply than physical abuse, especially for someone who has a sensitive, trusting, open heart. The wounds from verbal abuse can last a lifetime and result in low self-esteem or addictions, which are used to cover emotional pain.

— **How to handle this:** Verbal abuse is never okay in any circumstance. If the person calls you a name one time during a heated argument and then sincerely apologizes and doesn't repeat the behavior, this relationship may heal. However, if the verbally abusive behavior continues, you need to seek help and support from a trusted person, counselor, or support group. If the verbally abusive person is a parent or someone with whom you live, it's very important that you ask for help right away so that you don't develop deep-seated emotional scars. The sooner you receive help and support, the greater your likelihood of coming through this experience strong and healthy.

Rudeness

Inconsiderate people are always texting when you're trying to have a conversation with them, take another call when you're on the phone with them, and look at other people instead of you when you're talking.

— **How this relationship affects you:** If you're related to the rude person, you might feel emotional pain that his or her behavior signals a lack of love or respect for you. If the rude person is a friend or romantic interest, you may have fantasies about telling him or her off or leaving the relationship.

— **How to handle this:** Although you might argue that there's nothing you can do to change a rude individual, this is a perfect example of the fact that as an assertive Earth Angel, you are honest for the sake of honesty, and not in order to change the other person. You'll gain in personal strength and confidence by having an assertive and frank conversation about how you deserve and need respect and attention from the people in your life.

Betrayal

A betrayer breaks your heart and your trust by engaging in hurtful behaviors such as infidelity, flirting with others, lying to you, or exercising extremely poor judgment.

— **How this relationship affects you:** Since the foundation of relationships is trust, discovering betrayal is devastating. It makes you question yourself and your reality.

— **How to handle this:** For most people, betrayal is a deal-breaker. If it happens one time, and you feel the relationship is worth salvaging, you can both become closer as you analyze and work on the reasons why the betrayal occurred. You must be extremely clear and assertive and let the person know that he or she has hurt you, and that you'll not accept this or tolerate this behavior ever again. Know that you deserve relationships with people who honor commitments because they have high self-esteem and know that doing the right thing is part of taking care of themselves and the relationship.

Gossiping

A gossiper talks trash about everyone, and perhaps you have participated in that gossip with this person in the past. But then you discover that this "friend" is also gossiping about you behind your back.

— **How this relationship affects you:** You're surprised or even shocked that this person, who complains about everyone, is now complaining about *you.* You believed that you two were a united team who mutually found fault with others. You're left with feelings of disbelief and betrayal, and wonder how your judgment could be so off as to trust him or her.

— **How to handle this:** As with all other relationship issues, assertive honesty is healthy for you, although it may or may not change the other person. Someone who gossips is usually addicted to the drama it brings. So, since you now know that you can't trust this person, if you choose to continue this relationship, or you *must* because you're related to each other, you'll need to vigilantly guard against feeding the gossip. No more handing out juicy bits of information about your life. This means that you'll have to be guarded around the person, which will ultimately distance you from him or her.

P.S. Gossip is always hurtful, and any pain you have received from this relationship can be a valuable life lesson, teaching *you* to never gossip, because it only causes pain for everyone involved.

One-sidedness

In a one-sided relationship, the other person only talks about him- or herself, and never asks how you're doing. The minute you start talking about yourself, the other person leaves, ends the conversation, or pulls the topic back to him- or herself.

— **How this relationship affects you:** You feel unimportant, as if you don't matter. In this relationship, you'll feel lonely, and "not good enough" to warrant the other person's attention or affection. Until you catch on to the fact that this person is self-absorbed, you may chase after his or her attention and affection.

— **How to handle this:** One-sided relationships can go one of two ways: (1) In most situations, there's no possibility of relationship growth into a mutual friendship, because such people aren't open to hearing any dialogue except for the part they contribute. (2) In the rarer outcome, you have an assertive talk with the individual, telling him or her your honest feelings about how you value your relationship and you'd like it to continue under a new dynamic of equal sharing and equal listening. Ideally, the person will listen and be more sensitive to your needs in the relationship. But again, the point of being honest is that it's healthy, not that it will change the other person.

Drama Queen or King

With drama kings and queens, you spend hours on the phone, counseling them and giving them support; however, they never take your advice. Such people have one dramatic problem after another and only want to complain, without taking any steps to heal the situation.

— **How this relationship affects you:** This relationship leaves you feeling drained of time . . . and patience. In the beginning, you're flattered that this person is confiding in you. But soon, you catch on that the phone calls are never-ending sagas paralleling a daytime soap opera. That's when you start to avoid his or her calls.

— **How to handle this:** As an assertive Earth Angel, you have to confront the situation directly. Avoiding phone calls is a *passive* way of handling this. Complaining about this person to others is a *passive-aggressive* way of handling it. The only *healthy* way to deal with drama queens and kings is to tell them that you'll be holding them in your prayers and wishing them well, but you have a lot of responsibilities that you must spend your time on. And then stick to this.

Taking Advantage

Keep your wallet or purse close to you when you're with opportunists, because they're constantly trying to figure out how to get money, free gifts and lunches, and anything else that they can extract from you.

— **How this relationship affects you:** Confused, frustrated, and drained is how you'll feel around people who take advantage of you. They're experts at manipulating others into feeling obligated to pay for everything. Even though you may promise yourself that this time will be different, once you're with the user, your wallet starts to come out. You hear your mouth saying that you'll help this person with this or that.

— **How to handle this:** There are many games you could play in an effort to have a more balanced give-and-take relationship. However, remember that dysfunctional situations such as this one are opportunities to grow. So, once again, it's a matter of making an appointment to talk with the person directly and honestly. For example, you could say to this person, "Let's go to lunch on Thursday and catch up. Oh, and I'd love it if you'd treat me since I have bought the last five lunches." And then follow through on this. Stop paying for everything. When the waiter brings the final bill, don't automatically reach for it. If this is your true friend, he or she will still be in your life. If someone leaves you because you stop paying for everything, the person was never your friend in the first place.

Barbed Tongue

Someone with a barbed tongue insults you, but not directly. What he or she says hurts, but you can't exactly pinpoint why. This person gives "left-handed compliments," which are insults disguised as compliments. As an example: "You look so much better in that dress than the last time I saw you wearing it." *Huh? What does that mean?*

Such people usually have some very deep-seated hostility and jealousy, and they're classically passive-aggressive. Instead of directly talking to you about something that's probably ancient history by now and clearing the old anger with you, they're going to poke you with hurtful words under the guise of paying you a compliment so that you won't know that they're a hit-and-run artist with words.

— **How this relationship affects you:** You'll have an immediate physical reaction of pain when this person talks, because you can energetically sense that he or she is hostile. Yet you may feel confused, because your brain is trying to track the person's words, and they just don't add up or make sense. He or she may claim that "it's just a joke" or "you're too sensitive" if you say anything about his or her stinging words.

— **How to handle this:** If someone repeatedly barbs you with left-handed compliments, it's time to question whether this relationship can continue or not. If it's a close relative, such as your mother or sister, you'll always have that person in your life in some form. But this doesn't mean that you have to hang out with him or her all the time. Assertive Earth Angels always handle conflict directly with honesty and own their feelings without guilt or apology. So, an example would be to say to this person, "I don't believe you meant to hurt me with the words you chose to use, but that's what happened. I was hurt by what I heard you say." Or, as soon as the person says something hurtful, issue an immediate, honest reaction such as, "Ouch! That hurt!" The person may explain that he or she meant something entirely different than what you heard. If this is the first time there has been a miscommunication, you can discuss and resolve the situation fairly rapidly. However, if this is a chronic pattern *or* if the person becomes defensive or dismissive of your feelings, it's time to question or leave the relationship.

Nonstop Talking

When you have a conversation with big talkers, it's as if they never breathe. All they do is talk and talk and talk, and it's never your turn. If you say anything, your words are immediately run over and crushed by their dialogue, which is really more of a monologue. When this person calls, you could set down the telephone receiver and walk away. The person would still keep talking, because he or she is not cued in to the other person.

— **How this relationship affects you:** This type of relationship will leave you frustrated every time. Your need to be heard and listened to isn't being met. If this is a friend or distant relative, you'll probably find yourself avoiding him or her, especially telephone calls, which can be very uncomfortable and time-consuming with this type of person.

— **How to handle this:** Set the parameters at the beginning of each conversation by saying, "I only have fifteen minutes to talk before my next appointment," and then adhere to this strictly. Say, "I've got to go, love you, 'bye," and then hang up. If you wait for the chronic talker to give you his or her blessing that the call is ending, it will never happen. He or she will always say, "Oh, and one more thing." *You* must initiate and follow through with ending the call.

--*--*--

Be *very* clear with other people about your expectations for the relationship ahead of time. Your ego will argue with you, saying you can't tell others the truth or they won't like you. The real truth is that unless you speak *your* truth, you're nothing but an empty shell to other people.

※

CHAPTER TEN

PEOPLE AREN'T FIXER-UPPERS

*B*ecause Earth Angels are so intuitive, they can often see the potential within others. In fact, it's very common for Earth Angels to fall in love with other people's potential. They take on friends and lovers who are "fixer-upper" projects.

Earth Angels unconsciously decide, *I can polish this person's finer qualities and really make him a good person!* Some Earth Angels decide that they'll turn a prospective lover into their ideal husband or wife. Then they get upset when that person doesn't want to change!

It's not fair to enter any relationship, whether of a personal or business nature, with the hidden agenda that you'll fix or change that person. Everyone wants and deserves to be liked or loved for who they are (and that includes you, too). While everyone can use improvement, people don't want to be controlled or told what to do.

As Earth Angels, we're naturally trusting. We also have the ability to see the good within everyone. We love a fixer-upper project, and that often includes "collecting" people who we believe need fixing up. However, the truth is that nobody wants to be fixed or changed, even if it would improve their lives. If they do desire change, they want it on their own terms and not coming from someone else.

Your job isn't to fix or change other people. You can *help* other people. You can *heal* them and *pray* for them. But your job is to heal yourself and be the most loving person you can during your lifetime. Love means being honest with others in peaceful ways.

In love relationships especially, you'll be continually frustrated and disappointed if you think you can "turn a sow's ear into a silk purse" and transform an incompatible person into your dream partner. It's best to be up front with a new boy- or girlfriend about your needs and desires in a relationship. If your dream is to be married, have children, and stay home to raise them—then tell the person before you enter a committed relationship. Don't wait until your second anniversary to spring this news. It's not fair, and you'll both have wasted your time and endured needless heartache if he admits that having children isn't in his life plan.

Deal-Breakers

In all relationships, there are "deal-breakers," meaning issues, behaviors, or situations for which you won't stand. Common deal-breakers include:

- Dishonesty
- Betrayal

- Cheating

- Any form of abuse

You may have additional deal-breakers such as:

- Must be a nonsmoker

- Must have good hygiene

- Must be romantic

- Must make a certain amount of money

- Must have a fit physique

- Must be a good stepparent to your children

- Must not abuse drugs

- Must have a spiritual or religious beliefs similar to yours

- Must love cats [. . . and so forth]

If he or she doesn't have the deal-or-no-deal qualities you're seeking, the relationship is over. To you, there's no compromising on deal-breakers.

Yet for some Earth Angels, there's a secret deal she makes without letting her partner know. She secretly decides she's going to "fix" his deal-breaking habits and turn him into her ideal mate. She fantasizes that her love is so special that he'll give up drugs, gambling, womanizing, and other toxic behaviors.

When he resists or relapses, she gets angry and blames him, instead of realizing that he was always this way! She knew, going into the relationship, that he had these issues. So it's really a matter of accepting responsibility for her choices and then forgiving herself for making them.

Almost every week on my call-in radio show or at one of my workshops, a woman will ask me if her boyfriend or husband will change. She tells me he's violating her deal-breakers. She asks, "Should I leave him? Will things ever get better?" (Meaning: *Will he become the ideal man of whom I dream?*)

My million-dollar question to someone who asks me this is: "If nothing ever changes about him or in the relationship and it stays exactly the way it is now, would you be happy?"

I always hear a gasp of surprise in response to this question, and a pause. Then a shaky voice always says, "No." She has just realized that she has two choices: stay in an incompatible relationship or leave. She realizes that her entire relationship was built upon a fantasy that he'd magically change into a different person: *If he really loved me, he'd be like me. If he was my soul mate, he'd have the same outlook on life as I do.*

If they break up, hopefully she doesn't hang on to resentment toward him. It wasn't his fault that he was incompatible with her. That fact was revealed at the outset of the relationship! She just chose to ignore it, because she looked upon him as a fixer-upper project, which was never wise or fair.

If you ignore the red flags that the angels send you when you're about to enter a relationship, don't blame the angels or the other person when the relationship turns out to be unhealthy. You had your warnings, but you chose to overlook or ignore them. Perhaps you thought, *This time it will be different,* or *My love will change him.*

Next time you get red flags, please turn around and go the other way.

You're Not a Fixer-Upper, Either!

Earth Angels think that if they change, other people will be nicer to them. If they're sweeter, thinner, sexier, richer, more successful, prettier, smarter, better-dressed, and so forth, then they'll be accepted. They'll finally feel the big love that they remember feeling in heaven.

Changing yourself to win love is a desperate attempt to control another person's opinion of you! Let it go! Love yourself as you are, and only "improve" yourself because you're guided to—not to get someone to love you. In other words, make self-improvements because it makes *you* happy.

CHAPTER ELEVEN

ENJOY LIFE,
INSTEAD OF
PEOPLE-PLEASING

Why does everyone else get to have a fun, happy life, but not me? is the Cinderella-like complaint that Earth Angels frequently think to themselves. After all, an Earth Angel rarely complains aloud. To do so might make others uncomfortable.

Every spiritual path and religion touts the importance of helping others. And being helpful *does* lead to happiness. But there's a tipping point for everyone who feels that they're giving much more than they're receiving in return.

In a healthy relationship, both parties give and receive. It's impossible to make it completely 50-50. However, a healthy relationship encourages both people to air their true feelings if there's a giving imbalance. In a healthy relationship, you feel safe telling your partner about anything that's upsetting you. Your partner listens and shares his or her feelings in return. You negotiate as a couple to creatively resolve the situation in a fair way that both people respect.

In unhealthy relationships, one person rules and the other hides his or her feelings. The ruling person is very clear about the source of upsets, and usually points the finger at the other partner. Very often, Earth Angels assume the role of the "scapegoat," a person on whom everything is blamed. It's the scapegoat's "fault" if there isn't enough money in the family budget, the kids are being too noisy, or the jar of peanut butter is empty.

Earth Angels also accept the blame and say "I'm sorry" continually, even for things that aren't their fault. They assume that if someone's angry, it must be something they did.

The Earth Angel cowers before the angry person, giving away personal power and praying that the confrontation will end soon. This dynamic partly stems from past lifetimes. In each lifetime, our personality stays relatively similar. It's a myth that we bounce between being cruel and kind to balance our karma. That just doesn't happen! Kind people stay kind throughout lifetimes, and cruel people (unless they experience spiritual growth) stay cruel.

So, you've probably had previous lifetimes with similar personality traits of kindness, generosity, and a flair for spiritual divination and healing. In those lifetimes, spiritual healers and teachers were persecuted and often killed. During the Inquisition, everyone blamed tragedies upon "witches" (the generic name given to spiritual healers and teachers, even if they didn't practice witchcraft).

For that reason, you developed a phobia of being blamed, because blame was once a death sentence. You may have even been burned at the stake, stoned to death, or permanently imprisoned because people unfairly pointed to your spiritual gifts as the cause of famines, childhood illnesses, crop failures, and so forth.

Deep down, your soul recalls each lifetime's happy and painful lessons. If your body is twitching or flinching, you find yourself exhaling deeply, or you have "goose bumps" while reading this section, that's a sign that you suffered in this way.

In this lifetime, you've likely twisted yourself in knots to avoid blame. You anticipate everyone's needs with your supersensitive intuition, and then do superhuman work to ensure that everyone's happy . . . partly to escape the tyranny of being blamed! Your underlying reasoning (which may be unconscious) is: *I'm safe as long as everyone's happy.*

Martyr-Victim-Rescuer

Earth Angels are unhappy with unbalanced relationships in which they give far more than they receive. So, they feel victimized, used, and exploited by unappreciative people. No matter how much trouble they go to, other people don't reciprocate. Of course, if an occasional nice person *does* offer to help, the offer is refused. That's because deep down, Earth Angels feel needed and wanted when others make unreasonable demands. They also feel more in control when they're the ones doing all of the giving.

What our Earth Angel wants more than anything is appreciation, which she equates to "job security" and "love." The Earth Angel wants to be reassured that she's pretty enough, smart enough, and lovable enough. She craves reassurance because she hasn't yet learned how to give herself feedback.

When you rely upon others to define who you are, you've given them your power. You treat other people as a mirror that reflects back to you whether you're a "good person." If they're happy and pleased, you're a good person. If they're unhappy or angry, you're not.

Of course, that's not true in reality. But lifetimes of abusive conditioning have left hypersensitive Earth Angels feeling highly afraid.

The Angelic Martyr/Victim

If you're worried about "bothering" others, and you rarely request that people help you, you may be trapped in an Angelic Martyr/Victim cycle. This cycle means that you feel resentful that no one's helping you, yet you're not asking others for help. You may even say no when others *do* offer to help you!

Martyrs are those who deny themselves any pleasure in life, because they focus entirely upon others' needs. But then they punish the people they're helping with passive-aggressive behavior, which just increases, instead of reduces, anger.

This cycle stems from low self-worth, where you value other people's time more than your own. You may assume that they're too busy to bother helping you, and that they'd feel resentment if you asked for their assistance.

Could this be a projection of *your own* feelings of resentment? After all, wouldn't you love to have others help you? It would almost be better if they just dove in and lent a hand without first asking. Because when they ask, that's when you hesitate and usually say "No, thank you."

To turn this around, it's important to begin accepting other people's offers of help. The exception would be when you can sense the helpful person really has a hidden agenda such as trying to ingratiate him- or herself to you (make you feel that you owe him or her). But if a genuinely nice person offers assistance, being assertive means that you say "Thank you," and accept this kind gesture. Then, afterward, avoid the old habit of saying "Thank you" a million more times or apologizing for being a bother.

When you receive, the other person has the pleasure of giving. Allow him or her to have the inherent reward that accompanies helping another person (you). The other person will derive satisfaction from feeling helpful and useful. All humans have the need to feel needed. When you think of it this way, you'll agree that it's selfish to be the only one doing the giving. So spread the love by giving others the opportunity to give to you!

People-Pleasing

Your need for other people's approval puts them in control of your happiness. No one deserves that power over you.

You seek approval to avoid conflict. You have an uncanny sense about what other people want to hear, and you know how to feed it to them in heaping spoonfuls! Meanwhile, the other person believes that you're the nicest person on the planet—which you *are*, except there's an authentic and real version of your nice self masked behind "people-pleasing."

"People-pleasing" takes the phrase "If you can't say anything nice, don't say anything at all" to a whole new twisted level. It means that you're pretending to be someone different from who you really are, in order to control how another person reacts to you.

You try to prevent the other person from being angry with you, leaving you, or firing you by being extra-compliant and phony-nice. Or, the flip side is that you try to control others into liking you, marrying you, promoting you in the company . . . all by pretending to believe what they believe and laughing at their jokes and having a false front.

So people-pleasing is a dysfunctional and ultimately manipulative and dishonest way of relating to other people. There's nothing pleasing about people-pleasing!

You can be pleasant and very kind, thoughtful, and nice while still being genuine and honest with others. In fact, the most charming people are those who tell you the truth in a loving way. This is the combination for Earth Angels to aspire to: being real, nice, loving, *and* honest.

Everyone can relate to real human emotions. So when you admit how you really feel, it's a relief to people to know that others feel the same way they do. In this way, by being honest with others, you're being a teacher of how to live an authentic life.

Many people confuse being honest with being aggressive. That's because for so many years, the average nice person was passive and silent. But that has all changed, thank goodness! These days, it's essential for nice people to speak up about the issues that are near and dear to their hearts.

For instance, if your child is having difficulty with a teacher, it's very appropriate for you to hold meetings with either that teacher or the principal. This is an example of you taking action because you love your child. You speak up and are honest because that's the only way to protect him or her.

In personal situations, being genuine can bring blessings, too. For example, let's say that you and a group of friends go to see a movie. The movie is awful, and you don't want to watch any more of it. You look over at your girlfriends and they're squirming in their seats and seem to not be enjoying themselves either.

So, you whisper to the friend next to you: "I'm not enjoying this movie . . . are you?" Your girlfriend smiles with an expression of relief that you've put into words exactly how she feels. It turns out that none of your friends like the movie, but they're afraid to say anything and ruin everyone else's time. Because you had the courage to speak up, the evening is saved! You leave the movie early and go to a restaurant and enjoy a nice meal together instead.

If you were people-pleasing, you'd endure that movie because you wouldn't want to spoil other people's fun. But because you had the courage to speak up, you actually helped your friends.

And you'll find that this is the case in nearly every situation where you speak up. Again, speaking up doesn't mean aggression. Speaking up simply means that you *own* your feelings and state them clearly without blaming anyone else and without anger or sarcasm in your statements.

People-pleasing is a form of being controlling and manipulative. It stems from fear, not from love. People-pleasing comes from a place of unworthiness and undeserving feelings. You're convinced that other people won't like or love you if you show them who you really are.

Remember that you're a creation of God, made in the image and likeness of the Divine Creator! Everyone and everything that God creates has Divinity and inherent natural beauty and uniqueness. You are Divine!

It sounds counterintuitive, but you'll like yourself more when you're genuine with others. The more you can embrace your unique self and trust your passions and interests to guide you upon the path of your purpose, the more you'll find like-minded friends.

If you've been teased for being weird or odd, that's a sign that you have special qualities and uniqueness that the world needs. How drab and boring would it be if everyone was alike? And in some circles of people, it's an insult to be called "normal."

If you people-please, everyone will know it. People-pleasers never get away with their act. Others know that you're faking your feelings, laughter, and smiles, and they'll doubt your sincerity and your integrity. They won't trust you, and they'll wonder what else you might be dishonest about. So people-pleasing can sabotage your credibility in business, and your trustworthiness in relationships.

Pretending in order to be liked or to fit in with others never works! For one thing, it's exhausting to put on a front for very long. You'll find that you're absolutely drained of energy and enthusiasm from pretending to be someone other than who you really are. Plus, pretending detaches you from your real feelings. You'll *forget* who you really are after a while. You'll give up your true interests. And no matter how many friends you've attracted as your false self, you'll still feel lonely and unloved because they don't love you for your *true* self.

The only way to fill your heart is to take the risk of being your authentic self publicly, and then let nature take its course. The people who don't respect you aren't allowed to be in your life anymore. The people who are attracted to your uniqueness are possible friends, provided that you're also attracted to the idea of being friends with them . . . and they treat you with respect.

Remember that there's never been a person in history who was universally loved by everyone, so don't waste your time with this impossible goal. Be yourself and you'll attract like-minded people.

Other people can feel when you're being genuine and sincere. They'll relax around you and respect you more when you let go of trying to control their opinions about you, and allow your true feelings and natural reactions to shine. And you'll know that *the real you* is being loved and appreciated, which will increase your self-confidence and self-esteem!

※

CHAPTER TWELVE

KARMIC RELATIONSHIPS

*T*he relationships that drive you crazy with anger and frustration originate from a past life. These are the people who really get under your skin and exasperate you endlessly. Very often, these karmic relationships are with people in your immediate family.

Karmic relationships mean that you've had prior lifetimes with this person, and you both were sent back to be together to work things out peacefully. This was your soul's choice, although it was probably highly pushed upon you by your guides and angels, who helped you script out much of your life. Usually a karmic relationship is someone with whom you had a battle or shared other harsh circumstances. You returned together in this lifetime to ensure that you'd work things out, and clear both of your energies.

If you don't clear the energies in this lifetime, you'll be pressured to continue to incarnate with this soul again and again and again. And each lifetime, his or her relationship to you will continue to be close, either through genetics and familial bonds, or through friendship, marriage, or career. So, that annoying co-worker could be your mother or husband next lifetime unless you clear the energy with her in this one.

You're brought together with the other soul so that you can forgive him or her. This doesn't mean forgiving their actions. It means detoxing your soul by releasing anger toward them. You don't have to hang out with the person, but you do need to release old pent-up toxic feelings. Holding in old anger is caustic and unhealthy.

It's also a waste of time and energy to blame that person for family dramas and your own upset. Blaming is a projection of our ego, where we don't own our own shadows and ego issues, and we put them in the basket labeled: "It's their fault." And while it may be true that that person is the instigator of traumas, blaming him or her doesn't help the situation and doesn't balance the karma between you.

Karma and Earth Angels

Remember that you can't control or change any person except yourself. Your spiritual growth as an Earth Angel demands that you learn how to be at peace in the presence of annoying and infuriating relationships and circumstances. This is also part of your healing and teaching mission—to be a role model of how to walk through stressful and harsh circumstances with grace and poise.

To an assertive Earth Angel, the karmic relationship is like a final exam. It gives you the opportunity to test out all that you've been learning through this lifetime and have an impact through all subsequent lifetimes. It's the equivalent of the hero facing the dragon or the mortal enemy, and using all of his or her warrior skills at once. This is the exciting last scene from all action movies, where good triumphs over evil.

Sometimes it's helpful to do past-life work, such as a regression or asking your unconscious mind to give you a dream about your past life with this person. When you remember your past with your karmic-relationship person, it defuses the present-day anger. It helps you step back and detach from the current dramas.

You don't need to share the past-life information with the object of your karmic relationship, unless you feel strongly guided to do so. Talking about these types of issues may bring up even more unnecessary drama.

The next step in unraveling the tangled karma between you two is for you to understand that this isn't about the other person; it's about *you* and *your* spiritual growth and future lifetimes. Loving and caring for yourself means making an investment that helps you have more peaceful relationships now and in your future, including your future lifetimes.

As annoying as this karmic relationship is now, it will only become more intense if it's allowed to continue into the future. You have the power to stop the karmic wheel!

Breaking the Karmic Cycle

The first step to break this karmic cycle is for you to take responsibility for its presence in your life. Your soul agreed to be with this person because it was necessary for your spiritual progress. So forgiving yourself is the ultimate secret to healing everything in all directions of time.

This involves forgiving yourself for entering this relationship whenever you did in the distant past lifetime. You probably were given red-flag warnings by your angels then, which you chose to ignore or override. Forgive yourself for ignoring those red flags, and vow to listen from now on. Life lessons only count if we learn from them.

Yes, you're infuriated by the way this person behaves. But this is how this individual's personality works and has always worked. You were the one who chose to try to be in a relationship with him or her long, long ago. You were the one who decided that all of those red flags that your angel sent you didn't matter. You were the one who decided that you could change or fix the person.

Now it's time to let go of that fantasy that this person could be as you desire or dream him or her to be. You're not the other person's Source, nor are you the author of his or her life scripts.

Karmic relationships are akin to having a tug-of-war. They're power plays, where one person will pull and the other person will pull back. No one wins in karmic power plays. But when one person drops his or her side of the rope (through the process of forgiving him- or herself for getting into this tug-of-war in the first place), the power struggle stops.

Of course, dropping the rope and forgiving doesn't mean that you'll turn into a passive person. Remember, this is about *increasing* your personal power and assertiveness. In the past, you've tried aggressive, passive-aggressive, and passive processes within your karmic relationships. None of these have worked. Now it's time to be assertive, which means being honest with yourself and others. Honesty means that you let go of the agenda of trying to control, fix, or change the other person. Honesty simply means: speaking your truth, and letting the chips fall where they may without attachment to outcome.

Avoiding the karmic relationship (staying away from the person) can only work if you can get to a peaceful place inside your mind whenever you think of that individual. Your litmus test of whether you've balanced the karma is when you can see something that reminds you of the person and your blood pressure doesn't go up.

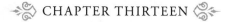
PARENTAL ASSERTIVENESS
WITH A
STRONG-WILLED CHILD

*E*arth Angels from the lightworker generation often have children who are indigos. Most commonly, lightworkers give birth to indigos, who in turn give birth to crystal children; and crystal children, as adults, give birth to rainbow children.

These are designations that aim to best describe the different characteristics of various generations:

- **Lightworkers** tend to be synonymous with our definition of *Earth Angels,* meaning those who are highly sensitive and yet out of touch with their true feelings and reluctant to share their truth openly.

- The **indigo children** are also highly sensitive. The big difference is that this generation comprises strong-willed leaders who are very outspoken about their feelings. Indigos have a well-developed truth detector in them, which can instantly tell them whether or not a person is sincere and if he or she has integrity. Indigos tend to have a temper, and an edge to them. They're natural-born activists who speak out about social and environmental issues.

- The next generation is the **crystal children.** These are even more sensitive people who are very connected to nature and animals, are highly artistic, have big eyes that stare, and rarely talk much. Crystal children are happy, sweet, quiet, forgiving, and very wise.

- The next generation is the **rainbow children,** who are still very rare at the time of this writing (2013). Rainbow children are essentially crystal children who talk a lot.

Lightworkers Raising Indigos

Of all these generations, indigos present the most challenges for parents. They don't respect anyone unless that person deserves respect according to the indigos' protocol. The indigo generation is here to dismantle corruption. Much as a drug-sniffing dog can detect narcotic paraphernalia instantly, the indigos can spot a fake or phony authority figure.

So an indigo won't respect their teachers, school principals, or other elders, unless the indigo feels that the person in question really has earned it. This ensures that the indigo will have many run-ins with authority figures, often pulling the parent into disciplinary meetings.

An indigo's parent (the Earth Angel) has an overwhelming need for everyone to be happy. That includes her beloved children. Indigos are extremely authentic and real with sharing their emotions outwardly.

Since indigos are so sensitive to corruption, and so much corruption still exists in the world, most are genuinely upset with the state of the planet, politics, the military, energy management, and so forth. So an indigo isn't happy! This confuses and confounds the Earth Angel parent, who's doing everything possible to *make* her child happy.

For instance, she is working two jobs to pay for everything that her child could want or need. She reluctantly agrees to whatever her son or daughter wants.

An example that I often hear about from Earth Angel parents involves violent video games. Most Earth Angels tell me that they're highly sensitive to violent movies, TV shows, and games. They're particularly sensitive to loud sounds from these media sources. And so they run into a conflict because their children enjoy violent video games, and may even be addicted to playing them.

Whenever the Earth Angel parent brushes up on the topic that she'd prefer to have no violent media in her peaceful home, the indigo child bluntly argues that he *needs* these video games. The strong negative emotions greatly trouble and frighten the Earth Angel parent.

So, many Earth Angel parents cave in to their children's desires, even if it violates the parents' personal boundaries (that is, their need to have no violent video games in the house).

Another example involves food. Many Earth Angels are sensitive to the food they eat, so they tend to eat very healthily. If an Earth Angel's child doesn't want to follow suit, the parent has two choices: to insist that while the child is living under her roof he'll eat a certain way; or to give in and allow the child to eat whatever he desires.

I find that Earth Angel parents who allow their children to do whatever they want live in a household that's filled with drama.

Strong-willed children secretly desire their parents to be stronger than they are. They need their mom or dad to step up and say the right thing, because the child knows deep down what the right thing is, too. Part of being an assertive Earth Angel is to muster up the courage to speak your truth and hold your boundaries, even if the other person is unhappy with your words.

When my very strong-willed son Charles was young, he respected my words because I would mean them when I said them. I always backed everything up with action, so he knew I wasn't bluffing.

The key to raising strong-willed children is that you must be stronger than they are. When Charles was young, I prayed constantly for God, Jesus, and Archangel Michael to give me strength. And they always did!

Many Earth Angels have had past-life relationships with their children from this life. Because our planet has such a long, tumultuous history, it's very common for Earth Angels to have had tragic or painful past-life connections with their children. A common scenario is where you lost your child in a past life, triggering excessive feelings of anxiety about your child in *this* life.

Because of this anxiety, Earth Angel parents tend to unconsciously overcompensate by doing everything humanly and angelically possible to keep their child happy . . . even to the detriment of both parent and child. All children need consistency from their parents as a top priority. Many studies show that when children can't predict their parents' behavior, it can lead to great insecurity that follows them into adulthood.

Children thrive under strong and clear parental guidance. They need their parents to step up and speak up. They need their parents to teach them healthful ways to deal with stress, relationships, boredom, and goals.

It's important not to be afraid of your child's disapproval! If you don't want violent video games, junk food, alcohol, foul language, and the like in your house, you have the right to say so and to enforce that boundary strictly.

Any boundary you have pertaining to your home and your child is natural and needs to be expressed openly. But that's not all: the most important part of telling your strong-willed child—or anyone else—about your boundaries is to have the courage to follow through in enforcing them, even if your child exhausts or upsets you while you're holding your ground.

Remember, Earth Angel parents: Your job is to shepherd and teach your child how to get along in the world after you're gone. Teach your child to be strong and to maintain his or her big, free spirit. Teach your child to be authentic and to step up as a leader and activist.

Your child learns from observing your behavior. Your child watches how you deal with stress. Do you turn to alcohol, food, pills, television, or other toxic, numbing habits? Or do you take healthful measures, such as attending a yoga class or going on a nature walk, when you're stressed? Your child will eventually mimic your behaviors.

Teach your child to respect you as the parent. Don't engage in power struggles. Anytime you have a power struggle with anyone, you're implying that someone can take your power away. You've already got 100 percent maximum power, and you don't have to fight anyone to get it back. You never lost it, unless you gave it away. And even then, you can't *really* give your power away, because God endowed you with it. And what God has created and given is eternal.

><

CHAPTER FOURTEEN

ASSERTIVENESS WITH AUTHORITY FIGURES

*Y*ou and I are one. You're one with every person who ever has lived, and ever will live, on this planet. Regardless of another person's spiritual wisdom, success, and happiness levels, you're one with, and equal to, that person.

God created *all* of us equal and equally gifted. Of course, everyone uses their gifts in different ways. Some people practice and polish their gifts, but everyone's *potential* and *inherent gifts* are identical.

As children, we're pressured to conform with the wishes and desires of authority figures and even punished if we don't. So as adults, we may fear authority figures. We may feel too intimidated by bosses, teachers, or celebrities to dare to speak up honestly and be ourselves with such people.

Fear always puts you into your ego. Your higher self, who's one with God and everyone, is never afraid. Your higher self is 100 percent love and light from the Divine. Your ego, in contrast, is 100 percent fear and darkness. So when you go into fear about authority figures, you're in your ego. It's that simple—for all of us!

It's as if life hands you a remote control with two buttons: one that says FEAR and one that says LOVE. Those are our two choices, in every circumstance of life. There are many shades of love, just as there are many shades of fear. But they always boil down to these two choices.

There will be many times in your life when you're called to be assertive with authority figures. This may be while you're doing activism work on behalf of an issue that's near and dear to your heart.

Perhaps, for instance, you'll need to speak directly with your local government representative to air your opinions about some initiative or law under consideration.

Or perhaps you need to speak with your boss about getting a promotion or raise, or introducing an idea for a new project.

It's normal for you to have physiological reactions to the stress and fear of facing an authority figure. This is hardwired into all organisms; plus, we're schooled for years to fear and respect authority figures.

A passive person never speaks up to authority figures, and rarely even looks them in the eye. The passive-aggressive person says angry words about authority figures behind their backs, and openly or secretly blames them for all of his or her problems. An aggressive person will confront an authority figure with loud and angry words or actions.

But an *assertive* person will speak directly to the authority figure with honesty, poise, and grace. Assertiveness is the way to create positive change, and also to put you on the highest vibrational level in all of your relationships. This includes your relationship with your Creator, angels, and loved ones; your karmic relationships; your relationship with authority figures, and most important . . . with yourself.

Beware of Pedestals

Sometimes the person you perceive to be an authority figure is someone to whom you're very close. It could be your parent; it could be your spouse. Earth Angels tend to put people up on pedestals. This means that because you admire the individual, you superimpose your fantasies of him or her being an ideal person.

The trouble with putting people up on pedestals is that they'll always fall off. And you'll be disappointed or even devastated when you realize they're human just like you. Every single person has an ego, including *you*. And the ego always leads you down a path of fear, fraught with mistakes.

The ego works through convincing you that you're separate from God, from angels, and from every other person. It does this by convincing you that you're either better or worse than other people.

When you put someone on a pedestal, you're automatically going into your ego because you're saying that this person is separate from you. Fear is the foundation of any relationship where you feel the other person is "less than" or "more than" you. And fear is an unstable foundation, guaranteeing a drama-filled relationship.

When you fear someone, you're giving your power to the other person. There are no authority figures in spiritual truth. There are only those who we have decided have power and control over us. Usually, that's because we've decided that we need that person's resources (such as money, prestige, connections, protection, approval, and so on). We've made him or her into a demigod, instead of seeing that God is the only authority figure and the only Source that brings us whatever we need.

Of course, it's fine to admire and appreciate people. But don't make them out to be separate from or better than you. Instead, let someone else's admirable traits inspire you to reach for your own dreams!

><

PART III

$\mathcal{B}$EING ASSERTIVE
OUT *in the* WORLD

CHAPTER FIFTEEN

FITTING IN
AND
WORTHINESS

*E*arth Angels feel like they're not a match with the rest of the world, like they've been dropped off on this planet and abandoned. It's as if they don't know the rules and just can't fit in anywhere. They live in a constant feeling of being odd, misunderstood, and judged.

Very often when they're young, Earth Angels are teased and taunted for being weird. This is tragic for highly sensitive children. They form a low opinion of themselves because everyone else tells them that they're strange and different—or treats them that way, so they develop this self-image. This leads to feelings of unworthiness, which will haunt Earth Angels for the rest of their lives if it's not confronted and healed.

Healing Unworthiness

Unworthiness means that you don't feel worthy of receiving the same goodness to which you believe everyone else is entitled. As a person who believes you're unworthy, you'll sabotage good as it comes to you. You won't have your sights set high enough. You'll expect the worst, so that's what you'll attract and create.

It's so essential for you to understand that you're entirely worthy! First, you were created by God. And God created you in the image and likeness of Divine perfection. Even if you feel the opposite of perfect, your Divinity is still intact. What God created perfect can never be destroyed or lessened.

Second, you're here for a very important purpose. You can feel that truth, even if you aren't sure exactly what the nature of your purpose is.

The emotional pain of unworthiness and loneliness can actually be your greatest teacher that takes you to new heights of spiritual growth and self-understanding. This does require you to feel the emotions fully, without numbing the pain through dissociation or addictive behaviors or substances.

Allow yourself to feel the depth of the existential pain of being on this planet and feeling alone and misunderstood, with no real connections to anyone. Recall all of the times in your childhood and adult life where your relationships were painfully lonely.

Notice how all of these painful and lonely moments connect together, because they're one continuous thread of the same story line. This story began with your physical birth, when you had to suddenly deal with this harsh and dense experience. At the moment you were born, you felt disconnected from God and Divine love, like a newborn baby searching for her mother's breast. You've been on a quest to seek that feeling of complete and pure love since your birth.

Acknowledging the Shadows

Instead of feeling like a victim or depressed or sorry for yourself because you're lonely, let this feeling empower you. By being completely truthful with yourself about your underlying feelings of existential angst, you necessarily will drop your defenses that have been keeping you from facing the feelings that have been there your whole life. The truth is that you've felt lonely, rejected, and misunderstood since you were born. You blamed yourself for being unlovable because you felt unloved. But you defended against realizing this, because your ego wants to control everything.

Your ego, like everyone else's, doesn't want you to discover the shadows of polarities here on Earth. In this physical realm, it is a world of contrasts and opposites: hot and cold, dark and light, wet and dry, soft and hard, good and evil.

One reason why you came to this planet is to experience those divergent opposites. So you may wonder why there's so much evil, pain, and suffering on this planet. And sometimes you may feel that God has forgotten you or isn't hearing your prayers.

The darkness on this planet is only because of the physical dimension, which has a plus side and a minus side. So everything has a positive and a negative pole.

Earth Angels are often afraid of acknowledging or spending time researching the negative pole of physical life. They resist acknowledging the shadow side of life, including the fact that there are people who act in very selfish and evil ways.

Earth Angels often refuse to see the ego within everyone, including their own human self. This is because heaven's angels look past the ego. Like a celestial angel, the Earth Angel wants to see only the good within everyone.

This is a very high-vibrational and admirable trait of Earth Angels. However, in this physical world it's important to acknowledge both poles. Every single person has an ego. Egos are annoying, enraging, and manipulative. *You* have an ego, too.

If you refuse to ever see the dark side of the polarity, you won't acknowledge your own ego issues. You'll only see darkness in other people's behavior, but not your own. You'll deny and project your own dark feelings, instead of learning and growing from them.

How can you heal and grow as a person, unless you acknowledge that there's some work to be done? The acknowledgment that there's work to be done isn't the same as saying you're unworthy or less than others.

CHAPTER SIXTEEN

PEACEFUL EXCITEMENT INSTEAD OF DRAMA

*Y*ou're already at peace, because you were created that way by the peaceful Creator. You don't need to look outside of yourself for peace, nor do you need to learn *how* to be at peace. You already have this inside of you at this very moment. Even if you don't *feel* like you're peaceful, you *are* in spiritual truth. In fact, it's impossible not to be peaceful in the universe as God created it.

If appearances seem to be otherwise, and you feel like you have a less-than-peaceful life, then this means the ego has been ruling the roost. What that means is that the ego has persuaded you that peace isn't valuable or attainable.

Peaceful Isn't Passive or Boring

The ego tries to tell you that peace is the same as being passive. It says that if you're peaceful, you'll lose your ambitious and hardworking ways, and you'll get behind in the competitive work world.

Nothing could be further from the truth! Being at peace doesn't mean that you become a slacker. It simply means that you're aware. You're aware of the Divinity in your oneness with all that is. You're aware of your honest emotions and opinions. And you're aware of your physical form and body and all of its feelings as well.

In business settings, a peaceful person always gets ahead. Again, being peaceful at work isn't the same as being passive or people-pleasing. Peaceful people are always assertive, because you have to speak your truth and be honest in order to retain your inner peace. Holding in your feelings takes you away from experiencing peace.

Peaceful people at work are also more open to receiving Divine downloads of brilliant ideas, which will be successful and appreciated on the job. Most people love to hang out with a peaceful person as well. That's because peaceful people have the attractive personality characteristics of being warm, approachable, open, and likable. They're pleasant to be around, and that's why they're invited to parties and committees, and given exciting opportunities at work. The old Hollywood-movie scenario of a hard, biting, harsh manager is a thing of the past. Nobody wants to work for or with someone who's obnoxious. They want to work with an inspiring leader. Peace and inspiration go hand in hand.

In personal settings, the same is true. Being a genuine person who honestly speaks your truth, coupled with an appealing personality that is accessible and lov-ing, is the ultimate winning combination.

~>—<~

Another reason why the ego pushes us away from being at peace is because it persuades us that peace is boring. This is another deception that has no basis in reality. Peace is its own form of excitement!

If you've been involved in roller-coaster dramas, you know how disruptive these experiences are to your daily schedule. Drama leads to obsessive thinking, where you focus on how angry, upset, or afraid you are. Fear and anger are two of the ego's biggest tricks, which it uses to pull us off the path of our Divine life purpose and peace.

So when the ego whispers in your ear that it would be very dull to have a peaceful life, don't fall for this! The ego tries to persuade you that high drama is exciting, fun, and meaningful. And while you can learn impor-tant life and spiritual lessons by experiencing painful occurrences, it's not the route to enlightenment.

Constant drama is so draining, and can even lead to emotional or physical health concerns. There's a steady supply of adrenaline and cortisol being secreted by your brain and your body during moments of fight-or-flight drama. This isn't healthy at all and can actually age you.

A peaceful life can be very lively! You can engage in stimulating activities such as sports, activism, or fun classes, and be peaceful and happy simultaneously. You can find thrills in all of the new opportunities that come your way as a peaceful person who's a magnet for others who want to work with you.

My life is simultaneously very peaceful and yet ex-citing. I am so honored and happy to be able to travel to wonderful destinations, and then meet the nicest people on the planet at my workshops. It's true that being peaceful can be *extremely* exhilarating and stimulating!

Getting Off of the Drama Roller Coaster

As with every other part of your life, you're in control of how much drama you experience.

You'll need to begin by taking an inventory, either by journaling or spending time alone with yourself in deep thought as you process in your mind how much energy you expend every day on your various activities. You'll be able to see how you're investing or not investing in your true priorities.

You may also want to keep a "drama diary" in which you record the drama that's swirling around you. Don't keep this journal near your bed, where its energy may disrupt sleep, but put it in a drawer when you're not using it so that it remains a detached tool to help you, and not an outline of your future life.

Notice any patterns in your drama-filled relationships. How much do you get back from these relationships versus how much you give?

How many hours do you spend on e-mail, text, phone, or in-person conversations with those who have endless complaints about their lives with no intention of fixing them?

How much time do you devote each day to putting out the fires of drama in your own or someone else's life?

To uncover your peace may require you to take some drastic actions. For example, do you feel that there are one or two people you're involved with who are instigators of drama? Again, review how much you're getting out of these relationships as opposed to how much you put into them. It may be time to cut back the hours you devote to a relationship that's pulling you off your path and probably draining your energy as well.

--&--

While your soul is always at peace, the rest of you may not feel peaceful. You may need to adjust your diet and lifestyle to exude more peace. This usually entails detoxifying from mood-altering chemicals and beverages. So that will mean that processed sugar, chocolate, and caffeine are off the list when it comes to your daily diet. For some people, this means a gradual detox, while for others, it's a cold-turkey process. You may want to work with a health professional such as a naturopath to supervise your detox, for maximum results.

Another form of detox that can help you experience more peace is detoxing from negativity and drama in the media and other parts of your life.

Decide to stay away from negative news, people who tend to speak negatively, and drama-filled reading material and television shows or movies. A long time ago, the angels told me that we're energetically affected by the media reports that we read. They taught me to use discernment in choosing magazines and newspapers.

One time when I was on a long airplane flight, I bought a bunch of magazines, including an issue of *People* (a U.S. celebrity-gossip magazine).

I was about to open the *People* magazine on the flight when I clearly heard the angels say to me, "By focusing upon other people's dramas, you attract more drama into your own life."

I gasped and closed the magazine. At the time, I was dealing with some upsetting drama in my life and definitely didn't want any more. I have avoided celebrity gossip ever since. And guess what? My life is now drama-free (yay!). I credit my discernment with respect to the media as a big part of my drama detox.

This may be a temporary drama detox, which you later decide is the best lifestyle for you. By keeping some distance from sources of drama, you'll definitely notice yourself becoming more detached and more at peace. You may need to actually go on retreat to a place where there are no televisions, cell phones, or Internet to effectively enact this drama detox.

Exercise and sleep also can contribute to feeling more at peace. Exercise is one of the ways to shake off excess adrenaline and help restore your mind and body to peace. When you exercise, it detaches you from the drama that's swirling around you. After a good workout, you wonder what you were upset about previously.

This is partially because exercise stimulates production of the brain chemical *serotonin,* which is a feel-good chemical that leads to feelings of peace and satisfaction. Serotonin also can help you sleep better and have an appetite for healthier foods and beverages.

❖—❖

Beware of the ego, which will try to pull you off the path of peace. Your ego loves endless drama, because it's filled with fear and anxiety. To the ego, drama is like candy, feeding its appetite for fear.

Drama can be another delay tactic or even an addiction so that you don't have to work on yourself or your life purpose.

If you have any thoughts of blaming someone or something else for why you're not at peace, you can bet that this is the ego's distraction at work. The ego always wants you to look outside of yourself for the reason for your unhappiness.

The calling card of the ego is blame or an outward focus. In contrast, the higher self (which is the true you) takes complete responsibility for itself. This isn't to say that you blame *yourself* at all. Again, *any* form of blame, whether directed toward yourself or others, is the ego's delay tactic and distraction.

Assertive Earth Angels are at peace and happy, no matter what's going on in their lives or around them. Even under the toughest and saddest of circumstances, they still feel the presence of God and peace within their hearts and minds.

Dealing with Selfish People

As we previously discussed, "drama queens" and "drama kings" are people who are addicted to the excitement of having a roller-coaster life. They love to get attention and be in the limelight of the center stage by having the world's worst problems. These are the folks who have all sorts of relationship crises, one after the other. They'll tell you this is because they have bad luck, and that they have no control over all of these experiences.

If you have a relationship with a drama queen or drama king, chances are it's a one-sided relationship. Usually, those who are constantly involved in drama have no time to listen to anyone else's stories. So, they'll spend hours telling you about their latest escapades, but the moment you try to turn the tables and talk about yourself, they have to get off the phone right then.

Drama queens or kings will never ask you how you are, except to get you to say, "I'm fine—how are you?" which is their cue to launch right into the latest episode of their ongoing saga. Ultimately, drama queens and kings are insecure, narcissistic, self-absorbed, and selfish.

I'm not labeling *them;* I am talking about their behavior. Everyone, including drama queens and drama kings and even the most annoying person you could ever meet, is a child of God just like you. Your higher self is one with their higher self. However, you'll notice that some people are completely acting out of their egos, while others have learned to tame them.

In fact, fear itself is the ultimate "diva" drama queen. Fear wants to be the center of your attention and distract you from your life purpose. So those who are drama queens or kings are allowing fear to control them.

If you spend too much time with people who are ego-centered, it will trigger your own ego to be louder and more in control of your day. And the ego is always the path to pain instead of peace.

One reason why Earth Angels are frequently hurt in their relationships is because they see only the good in other people. Of course, this is the spiritually best way to live. However, in this 3-D world of polarity opposites, the assertive Earth Angel also needs to acknowledge that some people's actions are dictated by fear and their egos.

Humans have a "selfish gene," and it's tied into aggression. So we have this old genetic predisposition to be selfish and aggressive, which served a lifesaving purpose in the distant past but is now fueling the very things that pose the greatest threats to humanity.

Taking Charge, Taking Responsibility

As long as you're blaming others for your problems, you'll always be controlled by them. Power comes from taking 100 percent responsibility for your life. It means acknowledging that everything in your current life is by choice. You may not have chosen your past, but you can choose your present and future!

It comes down to taking responsibility for your life. At first, this idea may seem crazy or frightening. You may misread this as my saying that others aren't causing you pain or blocks.

What I'm doing is taking away your "Victim Honor Badge," in which you continually think of yourself as a victim of controlling people and outside forces. Nothing could be further from the truth!

Do you really believe that our powerful Creator would make weak creations? Do you believe that God made some people more powerful than you? You might believe this if you define *power* as meaning a political title, wealth, education, popularity, fame, and so forth. But is that really power in the ultimate sense?

True power comes from deep within your core. It's David defeating Goliath with a tiny slingshot stone and huge amounts of faith.

CHAPTER SEVENTEEN

IT'S SAFE
FOR YOU
TO BE
POWERFUL!

*Y*ou don't need to become *more* powerful, because you already have 100 percent maximum power right now. Always remember that you're created in the image and likeness of the powerful Divine Creator. Therefore, you have all of the power of heaven within you, just like everyone does.

If you feel powerless and ineffectual right now, that's because you have made the decision that you don't have power. But that doesn't mean that it's so!

The spiritual truth is that nothing can take away the power that God created within you, ever! All it takes is for you to recognize and assume your power, and it's automatically enacted, to the point where you're aware of it and appreciate it.

Power is the same as assertiveness, by spiritual definition. It doesn't mean aggression, nor does it mean bullying or manipulating others. Power doesn't come from prestige, money, family background, or career.

Power comes from God, plain and simple. Since you can never be detached from this power, no one can block you from it—that is, unless you give it away. Giving your power away means that you wait to get permission from someone else before following through on your inner guidance.

As an example, let's say that you want to return to school to further your education related to your dream career. But you've put your husband on a pedestal as an authority figure, and you worry whether he'd give you "permission" to go to school. You worry whether you have the money, the time away from your family, and even the intelligence to complete your schooling.

See how you've just given your power away to others? Your desire to go to school is likely inner guidance that's Divinely directed, pointing you to your life purpose. By you going to school and gaining knowledge and confidence, all of your future clients will benefit.

If, on the other hand, you're thwarted from going to school because of fears of what other people may say, do, or think, then it is still within your power to make that ultimate decision.

Green Flags from Heaven

You're not a victim, nor can you ever be a victim. As long as you stay sober, alert, and aware of your inner guidance, you'll always be safe and supported. Just as angels send red-flag signs to warn you about getting involved with the wrong person, so do they send you green flags to direct you along the right path.

Green flags are when you get frequent and continual inner nudges to take positive steps or make healthful life changes.

Some women were raised with the notion that females are supposed to be demure and defer to a man's authority and power. This is so unhealthy and unnatural. Every person, regardless of the gender of the physical body in which he or she incarnated in this lifetime, has equal access to God's Divine power.

Several women have admitted to me that they equate power with manliness. They fear that they'll push men away from them by becoming powerful. But the happy truth is that it's entirely possible, and also admirable, to be both feminine and powerful. Power doesn't mean that you have to wear men's suits and go around bullying people. That's confusing power with aggression. They're not the same!

Power simply means that you honor your feelings, and have the courage to speak up about them without apology or trying to control the other person's reactions.

A powerful person is comfortable with him- or herself. A powerful person doesn't need someone else's approval in order to be happy. Emotionally healthy men and women admire and are attracted to confident women.

You already have these qualities, because you already *are* powerful. You may need to remind yourself of this if you're just beginning to reawaken and reassume your personal power.

It begins by questioning every part of your life where you've worried what other people will think. It means looking at any relationship where you're asking that other person for permission. It means being aware of whatever relationship triggers anxiety or fear within you.

A number of people have told me that they have a deep-seated fear of abusing their power, were they to allow it to be unleashed. Again, this is confusing power with aggression! Yes, it's true that when you're aggressive, you do abuse your authority. Aggressive people hurt others in order to get their own goals met. But a sensitive and loving Earth Angel would never dream of taking someone else's rights away or hurting anyone else in order to get ahead. This wouldn't even enter his or her consciousness. If you're the type of person who would abuse others, then you're no Earth Angel.

Some people are afraid of their power because it means that they'll be forced to take total responsibility for their lives, which frightens and intimidates them. But the positive truth is that when you take responsibility for your life, you then have control and power. This means no more blaming and no more playing the role of victim. It means that you stop asking permission to do what your soul is calling you to do, and you have the courage to take risks to change your life to match your dreams and inner guidance.

Perhaps your mother or father was trying to protect you by having you reel in your power. Perhaps you were a very strong-willed child, and your parents were frazzled because of their own lives, so they didn't have the time or energy to deal with your powerful ways. Perhaps you were shamed by others when you spoke up and told the truth. Others may have punished or abandoned you for being authentic. While such reactions from others can leave long-lasting emotional wounds, they don't take away your power. Again, nothing and no one can take away the power that God created within you. Your power is eternal and always at its 100 percent maximum intensity.

I believe that Jesus was trying to demonstrate for us that we're all connected to God, and that we all have this power. He said that all of us, with faith, can enact the miracles that he did—and more. It's time to stop playing "little"! Your life purpose could be the one to change the world and save the entire planet.

Delay Tactics

The ego doesn't want you to know who you are. It prefers to keep you shrouded in fear and insecurity, believing that fulfilling your life purpose is far down the road from today, and that you're nowhere near qualified or prepared enough to tackle it.

The ego is the tyrannical ruler within us all that wants everyone to stay in the dark so that it may be in charge and in control. The price we pay for its tyranny is that we don't explore the joys and the bliss of taking risks by following our inner Divine guidance.

So the ego uses delay tactics to ensure that you'll never quite be on your purpose. A delay tactic is any compulsive behavior that pushes you off your path. Delay tactics are distractions from feeling like you have the right, or enough time and readiness, to pursue your calling in life.

Your life purpose always involves love. And the form of love surrounding it is something that excites your interests, your sense of purpose, and your natural talents and passions.

So, for example, if you're crazy about animals and you love them almost more than life itself, that's a sign that your life purpose involves animals. Or if you find great pleasure in artistic or creative projects, this is a sign that your purpose involves creativity and artistry. If you love talking to people and helping them arrive at insights, your life purpose involves counseling or consulting or teaching.

If you feel frustrated or blocked in your life, channel those feelings in the direction of taking positive action steps! And don't allow anyone to tell you that you can't. When I first decided that I'd follow my inner guidance to become a published author, I mentioned this to my professor and supervisor in psychology. He immediately let out a guffaw at the idea and told me that I wasn't qualified to be a published author.

Fortunately, I didn't allow his laughter to stop me from pursuing my dream. I somehow summoned up my inner courage to write and submit my first book, even though my personal authority figure (my supervisor and teacher) tried to dissuade me.

Looking back now 25 years later, I can only imagine that his comments were because he didn't believe in himself and was projecting this onto me. If he had been a go-getter for *his* dreams, he'd naturally encourage other people to follow their own.

Sometimes people will attempt to talk you out of following your dreams because they're trying to protect you from disappointment. I promise you that whenever you pursue your dreams, there will be disappointments, but you'll overcome them! Disappointments aren't punishments in life; they're benchmarks showing your progress.

Never be afraid of failure or disappointment, because those are just temporary experiences on the path to your dreams coming true. Just because you fall, it doesn't mean that you'll stay down, unless you give up.

I personally have had many setbacks in my business and in my personal life along the way. I probably would have experienced setbacks anyway even if I *hadn't* pursued my dreams. But the happiness that I get from working on my dreams has given me the strength and endurance to survive those life setbacks.

As I mentioned before, when I first began writing books, my children were very young and I had a full-time job as a secretary. I went to college part-time during my lunch break. I was extremely busy! I could have easily said that I didn't have time to write my books. And no one would have blamed me. But I went ahead and did it anyway, because the thought of not pursuing my dreams was more terrifying than the thought of failing if I did so.

At first, I allowed my own ego fears to get to me. Instead of writing, I let myself be delayed by focusing on housework. I had this unconscious belief that I was not allowed to pursue my own dreams until my house was perfectly clean. I justified this by saying that my sons were very little and I didn't want them to come into contact with germs.

So I'd clean the carpets incessantly until all the dirt was gone in every single spot. I'd clean under and on top of the refrigerator daily. In other words, I was overdoing the housework. Although it's important to have a sanitary kitchen and home, I was clearly using housework as a defense against ever getting started on my writing. In that way, I was ensuring that I'd never succeed, nor would I ever fail or face disappointment if my book didn't get published.

Once I realized what I was doing, the unconscious fear rose naturally to the surface, where I could face it. Facing your fears is the key to overcoming them!

So what are *your* fears? Take a moment to confront them, and see that they really originate from childhood nightmares that have no real power over you at all.

Addictive Delay Tactics

Delay tactics are usually behaviors that you engage in compulsively as a way of atoning for your fears. Common ones Earth Angels use include:

- Overeating
- Substance abuse
- Addictive Internet surfing
- Compulsive shopping
- Love addictions

One little-known and insidious delay tactic is rescuing a friend. This involves spending one hour or more per day on the telephone listening to your friend's latest problems and dramas. Now, I should mention that this particular friend always has a brand-new batch of drama and troubles. Oh, and I should *also* mention that she has no intention of healing her life. She is only calling you to brag about how special she is because she has all of these amazing problems. She's calling because you listening to her validates her way of existence. She's using you as a delay tactic of her own, because as long as she's embroiled in one drama after another, she has the excuse of having no time or energy to focus on her life purpose.

You can give this friend all sorts of wonderful advice, but she'll never follow it or put it into action. She will always give you a "yes but" excuse for why she can't take your advice.

This really isn't a friendship, unless she's willing to listen to *your* problems after she's done discussing hers. Usually this type of friend is a drama king or queen (see the previous chapter and the earlier one on toxic relationships), who's seeking a sounding board or someone who will define him or her. You don't need one-way relationships; they're toxic and disempowering. So to break the cycle of this delay-tactic relationship, you'll need to admit to yourself this powerful truth:

You're using the friend as much as she is using you.

You're using this relationship because it's serving a useful purpose as a delay tactic. You can justify not working on your life purpose because you're too busy helping your friend through her problems. But when you get honest with yourself, you can see what a time waster this agreement is that you both have unconsciously made.

This type of continual drama and one-sided relationship needs to either end or be managed. Your top priority should be taking care of your physical, mental, and spiritual health so that you can be a vital member of the community and there for your family.

And part of taking care of yourself includes devoting at least one hour per day, without exception, to focusing upon your passions, priorities, and purpose (which are usually one and the same).

Being assertive means being honest with yourself and others, as we've emphasized throughout this book. That entails having the courage to face your addictions and other delay tactics. If your addiction is completely out of your control, seek professional help, including the online and in-person free support groups through Al-Anon and Alcoholics Anonymous. There are 12-step meetings for nearly every addiction, including eating disorders, compulsive spending, codependent relationships, and substance abuse. There are even wonderful and free-of-charge online 12-step meetings that you can easily find through an Internet search for "online 12-step meetings."

Many of these addictive behaviors are actually attempts to gain more happiness and peace. The ego tells you that if you acquire one more glass of alcohol, one more new dress, one more new relationship, one more cigarette, and on and on . . . then you'll finally be happy and at peace.

Be honest with yourself about how this delay tactic has done the opposite, and has actually *interfered* with your happiness, health, and purpose. Have a conversation with your delay tactic and tell it good-bye. Be willing to forgive yourself and everyone involved in enabling your delay tactic. Your sense of humor may even make you see that your delay tactic was part of our human foibles and quirks.

Every experience you've ever had has been a teacher and an opportunity to learn and grow. So all of the delay tactics that you've been involved in have taught you something and brought you blessings, even if you can't see them right now.

The purpose of delay tactics is to prevent you from moving forward. Delay tactics are your unconscious mind's and ego's way of preventing you from ever experiencing rejection, or disappointment regarding your dreams. Delay tactics allow your dreams to be perpetually in a state of suspension, where you'll never have to face the pain of having them not come true if you were to try for them.

But dreams, like lottery tickets, can only succeed if you take a chance on them. And then each day devote at least one hour toward *realizing* them. It doesn't matter *what* you do, but only that you do something—anything—related to your dream.

Love Addictions

Believe it or not, you can get addicted to love! Not the Divine love, which is 100 percent healthy, but the falling-gaga-head-over-heels type of love. Earth Angels are susceptible to love addictions because of their penchant to search for the bliss of heavenly love and their romantic desire for a soul mate.

Love addiction means that you continually look for "the one" so that you can have the fairy-tale romance that you dream of. You become hooked on the endorphins and neurotransmitters associated with romance, such as *phenylethylamine* (PEA), the feel-great chemical that your brain secretes when you're falling in love. This is the same chemical in chocolate and is in the same class as the drug ecstasy. PEA makes you feel like you're floating on air.

The other addictive chemical associated with love is called *oxytocin,* a hormone released when a woman is sexually aroused. This hormone emotionally bonds her to her partner. This is one reason why women can't have casual sex: oxytocin makes them want a serious relationship with whomever they sleep with.

Love addiction can be dangerous if you get involved with violent or inappropriate people in your quest for the addictive love feelings and chemicals. It can also lead to sexually transmitted diseases and low self-esteem and shame.

If you believe you may have a love addiction, you can gain real help from the 12-step group called SLAA (Sex and Love Addicts Anonymous), which has free online support to help you detox from inappropriate relationships. SLAA is based on the same effective model as Alcoholics Anonymous that has helped millions of people. Just visit www.slaafws.org to find resources and online meetings.

Perfectionism and Paralysis

If you have perfectionistic tendencies, you may try to delay working on your dream until you believe it's the perfect moment. This guarantees that you'll never move forward on the path of your purpose. Because—let's face it—there's never an ideal time for you to begin working on your dream.

Your ego will try to tell you that you must first feel ready before you can start. But the truth is that the ego will *never* allow you to feel ready, because it will always feed you lies filled with insecurity and anxiety.

Your ego will try to convince you that you're unprepared, unqualified, or a fake or phony.

In fact, one of the ego's favorite delay tactics is called the "Impostor Phenomenon." This means that you compare yourself to everyone else, using the ego's separation beliefs that you're less than others.

The ego will try to tell you that you're not qualified, or that you're an impostor who's faking your way to success. It warns you that you'll eventually be found out as a fraud, and all of your hard work will have been for nothing.

If you listen to the ego's warnings about being an impostor, you'll be paralyzed under the misguided notion that you're protecting yourself. You'll be afraid to make the first move, because you unconsciously remember your childhood or other lifetimes when you were ridiculed (or worse).

There will never be a time when you feel completely prepared, qualified, or ready. That's because such a time doesn't exist. You're always improving yourself and your life. There will always be some sort of issue or drama trying to pull you off of your path.

There's always some world crisis or some upheaval concerning a loved one, and these are ways for you to feel perfectly justified in focusing on *them* instead of upon your dream.

This goes back to what I've said repeatedly: just one hour per day, devoted completely to your dream, will be the genie in the magic lamp that grants your wishes.

If you feel like you don't have one hour a day, let's look at that belief. Perhaps you're tired in the morning or at night, and the rest of your day is devoted to work or other duties. What this means is that you simply must increase your energy levels so that you have more time available to you each day. This doesn't mean pumping yourself full of caffeine or other drugs to try to artificially stimulate your energy.

Your energy must be naturally stimulated through exercise, sunlight, and a healthful diet. By investing the time to exercise and eat healthfully, you will be rewarded with many extra hours of useful time each day. And that extra time can go toward daily work related to your life purpose. (In Chapter 19, we'll talk more about how you can increase your available time and energy.)

If you don't know what your life purpose is, you're not alone! For now, focus upon what you do know. You *do* know which activities bring you great pleasure and spiritual growth. So, spend this time focused on these activities.

Remember, always, to be your own authority figure with your schedule. You don't have to ask anyone for permission to have one hour a day for yourself. Give *yourself* permission and the authority to devote time to doing the writing, researching, creating, or other activities related to your intentions and passions and purpose.

Your power in your life is felt when you release everyone and everything that's a time waster and energy drainer. Examine every part of your life, and question what it brings you. If you have an endless series of relationships and situations where you're the only one who gives and who cares, take a look at that. Why do you choose to have such an unbalanced proportion of giving and receiving in your relationships?

Sometimes we choose unbalanced, one-way relationships because it makes us feel in control. If we're the ones who are doing all of the giving, then we can feel like we're calling the shots in the relationship. Perhaps being with someone who has a life full of drama makes us feel better about ourselves by comparison. Or maybe it feeds into the gossip rumor mill that we like to be a part of to feel special.

But remember the double-edged sword of feeling special. When you feel better than someone else, you're in your ego. It's very black-and-white. If you feel you're better or worse than another human being, you're in the ego mode of separation thinking.

The only route to peace, and the only escape from the ego's tyranny, is through continuously training your mind to know that you're one with everyone.

Of course it's fine for you to get compliments and feel good about yourself, because that's part of self-care and self-love. When someone gives you praise, it's also thoughtful and kind for you to accept it as the gift that it is. Be gracious, and don't deflect compliments back. To do so is the equivalent of refusing a gift that someone's giving you.

Never, ever put yourself down, in jest or seriously. When you say mean things about yourself, it's often because you're trying to manipulate or control someone else's pity or guilt toward you. This may even be an unconscious process.

The words you say about yourself are registered in your unconscious mind, where they affect your self-esteem and self-confidence. It's essential that you only use positive words and phrases when describing yourself. You can be very humble while also feeling good about yourself. Humility means that you honor and respect yourself and others, which is very different from self-deprecation, where you put yourself down for not being enough.

Getting Comfortable with Your Power

Watch young children or animals interact, and you'll see examples of honest assertiveness. You'll notice that animals and children have no qualms about making their needs and feelings known. That's because it's natural for all creatures to express themselves.

As with any new lifestyle practice, you'll become increasingly more comfortable with your personal power. At first, you may feel awkward or even like an impostor as you speak up for yourself directly and with honesty. You may be waiting for the other shoe to drop, in terms of expecting someone to call you out or punish you for speaking up. You may reawaken phobias from your school days, when you weren't allowed to speak unless you were given permission.

But with each small and large success that comes your way from speaking up, your confidence and comfort with being powerful will increase.

Remember that power is natural. So as you allow yourself to become more powerful, you're actually being your real and natural self.

✴

PART IV

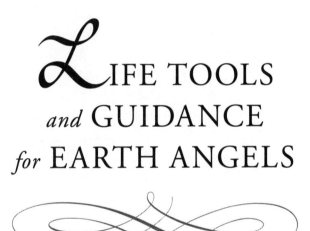

LIFE TOOLS
and GUIDANCE
for EARTH ANGELS

CHAPTER EIGHTEEN

ENERGY WORK FOR EMPATHS

*A*s a highly sensitive person—also known as an *empath*—you feel everyone else's emotions. Your body functions as a vibrational instrument, like a drum vibrating in tune to other people's thoughts and emotions.

As a sensitive Earth Angel, you also absorb other people's thoughts and feelings. This is why after you have a conversation with someone, you sometimes walk away feeling drained or upset. A part of this is because you're worried about whether the person will be okay in enduring a problem situation he or she is involved in.

Or you may be worried whether that person likes you or is mad at you, which is a very common concern that Earth Angels have.

You may even overcompensate to make sure the other person isn't angry with you by overgiving to that individual in a way that is out of proportion with your relationship. If you tend to be overly generous, especially with people who don't get back to you, this is a sign that you're feeling anxious and insecure.

It's also sign that you're carrying other people's energy, and it's confusing you.

Shielding

Shielding is like using an umbrella when it's raining. It's just common sense, and has nothing to do with fear or paranoia.

Shielding means protection against harsh, negative, or lower energies. Shielding yourself is a way to ensure that your energy stays high and clean, especially if you are traveling through or working in a harsh environment. For example, if you're employed at a company that has a lot of competition, political gaming, or negativity, this will affect you. Similarly, if you live with someone who tends to be negative, you will absorb his or her energy unless you have shields up.

Here are some ways to shield:

Crystals

Crystals are powerful minerals, rocks, stones, and gemstones that transmute, protect, and magnify various energies. Wearing, sleeping near, or holding these protective crystals, or placing them on your desk, can help deflect negative energy. Some of the more powerful shielding crystals include:

- **Amethyst:** This gorgeous purple gemstone helps lift the energy around you and in you.

- **Obsidian:** This beautiful black stone deflects negativity, anger, and psychic attacks.

- **Citrine:** This lovely pale yellow stone helps increase positive energy and push away negativity.

- **Clear quartz:** This beautiful clear crystal refracts sunlight into rainbows, and does the same thing to negative energy, breaking it up and turning it around.

- **Smoky quartz:** Put this brown crystal near your bed and you'll release negativity from past relationships while you sleep.

- **Rose quartz:** This pale pink crystal helps protect you in romantic relationships.

- **Lapis lazuli:** This beautiful blue stone is a good general protector.

Angel Lights

You can ask Archangel Michael, the protector angel, to shield you with his royal blue and royal purple light. To do so, just say either aloud or silently: *"Archangel Michael, please surround me with your protective shield now."* Because this archangel is unlimited, he is able to shield everyone who calls upon him instantly.

You can also ask God to send extra guardian angels to protect you; your loved ones; your home; your vehicle; or any other person, place, or thing. There are an infinite number of angels, and all we have to do is ask for more and it is done.

Clearing

Just as important as shielding is clearing your energy. Whenever you feel tired, get confused, or become accident-prone, take the time to clear your energy. A lot of times, these are symptoms of having absorbed negativity.

As with shielding, there are many fine ways to clear yourself. My favorite is to say: *"Archangel Michael, please clear away any energies from within me and around me that are not of God's love and light."* The archangel will immediately come to the aid of anyone who calls upon him, since he loves us all and has the ability to help everyone simultaneously.

Another way to clear is by taking a very warm bath filled with sea salts (which you can buy in the spice section of your local natural store). You can also add pure flower essences and essential oils to your clearing bath and surround the bathtub with white candles as focal points for your intention to clear yourself.

Massage or similar bodywork also has wonderful clearing abilities. This is especially true if you work with a massage therapist who is skilled in releasing energy, along with physical tension.

Detoxing your diet is another way to clear away physical as well as energetic toxins. You can do a juice fast, or work with herbs and supplements that flush out heavy metals and other physical contaminants that may be attached to energy toxins in your body. Talk to your local naturopath, or a trained individual at a supplements store.

Grounding

Grounding means that your consciousness is housed inside of your body, as opposed to floating above it, where you're not aware of what you're physically doing.

Many Earth Angels leave their bodies because they can't handle the earthly plane. They "go home" in their consciousness and aren't really here. This is okay to do during dream time or meditation, but during the day and waking hours, we must remember that we are in physical bodies for a reason.

To ground yourself, you can wear the crystal obsidian. You can also eat vegetables that grow in the ground, including organic non-GMO radishes, potatoes, carrots, onions, and turnips.

You can also ground yourself with a foot rub, either one you give yourself or one you receive from someone else. Another successful grounding technique is to visualize roots coming out of the bottoms of your feet, as if you were a tree. Feel the energy of the earth connecting with the bottoms of your feet.

One of my favorite grounding methods, though, is to connect with nature. Taking your shoes off and physically touching the grass, soil, sand, or water will help focus your mind back on your physical reality.

Trees Are Amazing Healers!

For shielding, clearing, and grounding, you can receive a lot of support and help from trees. I've always felt a close connection to trees. They "speak" to me, and I can hear and feel their energy and messages.

The trees taught me about their healing power. One time when I was traveling and had a backache, I was guided to lean against a tree. I could feel the pain being absorbed by the tree. The tree didn't hang on to the pain; it transmuted it.

Very quickly, my back felt wonderful!

Since that time, I have worked with trees for transmuting emotional pain and illness, too. I've also taught other people to do this, with the same positive results—including taking groups to connect with trees.

To heal with a tree's assistance, walk among a grove and mentally ask one to help you. Trust your inner guidance about which tree to work with. It will answer and call to you. You'll feel the response from the tree in your body and mind. I can hear an actual voice in my mind, as can many other people.

Then lean your back against the tree, and close your eyes and breathe. Be willing to let go of everything painful. And don't worry—it won't hurt the tree. It's the same process that trees have mastered to turn dirty air into clean oxygen.

Tree healings are remarkable, gentle, and very loving. Trees hold so much wisdom! Each has its own personality and special focus. No two are alike.

I also love sitting beneath trees and writing their messages. I did this in my book *Healing with the Fairies*, when the trees taught me about letting go of the past.

⊰—⊱

You can also clear and shield the world of negativity, which is a powerful process that all Earth Angels can engage in to help everyone who lives on our beautiful planet. Visualize the world being cleared and shielded, and ask God to surround the earth with extra guardian angels and protective light. The more of us who do this, the more protection the planet receives.

CHAPTER NINETEEN

HOW to HAVE MORE TIME and ENERGY

*L*et's face it: As helpful people, Earth Angels have very full and busy lives. We volunteer to help out different people and organizations because we have this natural impulse to offer our support.

So our busy lives may drain us of time and energy. What's an Earth Angel to do?

The easiest way to have more *time* is to increase the amount of *energy* that you have. When you have more energy, it gives you more useful hours during the day. Instead of experiencing a "crash" right after dinner, you'll find that your energy stays high until midnight. And then you have a sound night's sleep and wake up ready to go again with happiness and joy at 6 the next morning.

High energy is also a secret of rapid manifestation. The more you visualize, affirm, and pray for your dreams to come true, the higher your energy, and the faster your manifestation will come about.

So one reason why you continually get inner nudges from your guardian angels to live a healthier lifestyle is because they know that this will help all of your prayers to be answered. When your angels guide you to exercise, for example, they're not suggesting this because they're judging you or trying to ruin your fun. The angels know that daily exercise leads to a major increase in personal energy levels. Exercise allows you also to dissipate stress and let go of grievances that are distracting you from your purpose.

Even 20 minutes of exercise has been shown to significantly boost your levels of serotonin, which is the brain chemical that's secreted to help you regulate energy, moods, and appetite. The more serotonin you secrete, the better you feel.

Stretching and Releasing

Stretching your muscles daily is one easy and quick way to keep your body energized and limber. You can even do this in bed by lying on your back with your knees up and together. Then, with your arms down by your sides to balance yourself, move your coupled knees to your left and hold them while your muscles release and relax. Then, do the same with your knees falling to your right side.

Next, straighten your right leg and twist gently while you move that leg toward your left arm. Do the same with your left leg twisting toward your right arm.

Many painful emotions are stored in the hips and can be released by hip-opening stretches. For instance, lie on the floor near a wall. Scoot your hips close to the wall and then put your feet up on it. Open your legs as widely as is comfortable, and hold this position.

You may be surprised by the emotions that surface as you open your hips. Allow tears to spill and memories to surface. This is part of the releasing and cleansing process. If the emotions are too strong to handle, consider getting support through a group meeting or a professional counselor. Journaling about your feelings is also helpful during the releasing process.

There are many excellent free instructional videos about stretching exercises available on sites such as YouTube. Or you can take yoga or Pilates classes to get personal supervision as you learn safe ways to stretch your muscles.

Earth Angels and Weight

Exercise also helps you keep off the pounds. Since almost every Earth Angel struggles with his or her weight, this is important.

Because the earth is one of the harshest environments from a physical, energetic, and emotional standpoint, Earth Angels carry extra weight to shield themselves. This is the only planet that has such full-on competitive energy. Only on Earth is there a competition daily among people and animals who perceive that there's a lack of resources.

Earth Angels aren't very competitive, because they want everyone to win and be equally happy. So they're reluctant to jump into the *I must get ahead* attitude that prevails at so many companies and schools. Earth Angels know that life is meant to be a win-win condition.

Competitiveness, violence, and the other harsh energies of the earth are very foreign and disturbing to Earth Angels. They use food and alcohol to numb their sensitivity levels. And the extra weight that they gain physically helps act as a buffer against the harsher energies.

The two-part trouble with this is:

1. Earth Angels are highly sensitive to chemicals that they ingest. They are very prone to allergies. So by indulging in toxic foods, beverages, or drugs, they reduce their energy levels and also may experience inflammation, anxiety, or depression from those substances.

2. The second part of this equation is that Earth Angels are highly sensitive to what other people think about them. They're susceptible to soliciting other people's approval as part of their desire to make sure that everyone is happy. Earth Angels know that they're not originally from this planet, and they feel like outsiders who are struggling to fit in.

So, the extra weight that Earth Angels carry on their bodies may make them subject to other people's disapproval. After all, there's a lot of pressure to be slender and fit in this world for both women and men. Of course, it's best for our bodies to be at a healthy weight, but the pressure to be extremely thin for women and extremely muscular for men makes Earth Angels have self-doubts about their worthiness in this world.

Many Earth Angels judge themselves because they don't have a perfect body. And they use this self-judgment as a way to block themselves from going out confidently in the direction of their dreams and life purpose.

But the truth (and I am now speaking as a former eating-disorders therapist) is that no one feels 100 percent good about their body in this world. Everyone can point to some part of how they look that doesn't conform to the unnaturally thin and perfect models in the media. Those models often have tragic eating disorders in order to stay so thin. Only about 10 percent of the population can eat whatever they want and stay model-thin. Their photos are also digitally enhanced to give them perfect skin and figures.

So Earth Angels who take care of their bodies by eating healthfully and exercising daily will have more energy and higher self-confidence.

As an Earth Angel, you tend to take on other people's troubles. You may even encounter situations where strangers approach you and tell you all of their problems. That's because people can intuitively trust you. And if this happens to you frequently, it's a sign that your life purpose involves counseling others professionally.

Let's ask for Divine help. After all, sometimes Earth Angels forget to "phone home" and ask for assistance.

There's no one-size-fits-all universally healthful diet or exercise program that will work for everyone. Everyone's energy metabolism is different. But one thing is for sure: everyone has guardian angels who know exactly the right exercise and diet program for that particular person.

Most likely, you've been receiving strong intuitive guidance to make healthful life changes in your exercise, sleep, and diet routines.

If you're like most people, you've been resisting those urgings because you don't want to let go of the entertainment, pleasure, and convenience of your current lifestyle choices. You may resist being told what to do, even if it's angels who are giving you this guidance as an answer to your prayers.

So let's ask God and the archangels what they're guiding you to do as far as eating, drinking, and exercising are concerned. Let's make their guidance clear and conscious right now.

Take a moment to notice your shoulders, and as you breathe, ask them to relax. Continue breathing and asking your other muscles to relax. Inhaling deeply, center your focus in your heart and think about angels. As you do so, you're calling your angels to help you.

Then say this question to your angels either aloud or silently: "Dear guardian angels, what changes would you like to see me make in how I treat my body?"

What's the first thought, feeling, words, or visions that just came to mind as you read and posed that question to your angels? Most likely, it's the same guidance that you've been receiving and dismissing. Perhaps you've been procrastinating or ignoring this guidance.

Remember that your angels are on your side. They aren't trying to control you or ruin your fun.

Next, please say the sentence out loud:

"Dear angels, please give me clear signs that I can easily notice and understand to help me know that I have correctly heard you today. Please give me the courage, strength, and motivation to enact these healthful changes without hesitation or delay."

If you have any medical issues, you may also want to research healthful diets with a nutritionist, naturopath, or holistic doctor.

The sooner you make the changes as you're guided, the sooner all of your dreams will come true.

Let's ask Archangel Raphael, the healing angel; and Archangel Michael, the angel of courage and protection, to assist you:

"Dear God and Archangels Raphael and Michael, please help me to only crave healthful foods and beverages. Thank you for giving me the motivation, time, support, and encouragement to exercise my body daily. I now surrender to you all of my previous fears and excuses about taking better care of my physical body."

CHAPTER TWENTY

ANGEL ACTIVISTS

*D*on't be a lazy lightworker! Pull your weight, get to work, do your share, and help the rest of us. There are real-world issues that need your attention, now!

If this world were perfect, you and I wouldn't be needed here. We could have just stayed home in heaven and sent prayers from above.

A passive Earth Angel lets the government do what it wants, a passive-aggressive Earth Angel complains about the government, an aggressive Earth Angel may act out violently against the government, and an assertive Earth Angel stays aware and gets involved and speaks up.

You can read the news to stay abreast of world and local events through your Earth Angel lens: First, know that the "news" is someone's opinion of what's happening. Each newspaper will report the same story with differing slants. Many newspapers are corporate owned, and reporters are ordered to write biased reports that favor particular financial and political agendas.

Look upon news pieces as "Divine assignments." Rather than worrying about a story or allowing it to upset or depress you, pray about it instead! By sending prayers to the situation, you *are* helping. When Earth Angels get upset, they emit powerful toxic energies into the atmosphere. It's important to channel those real human emotions in constructive ways.

I am so proud of Earth Angels who take the time to read alternative and mainstream news, including watching videos and documentaries on YouTube, Hulu, and other Internet video sites. I am proud of Earth Angels who are aware of the issues facing our planet right now! And I am especially proud of those of you who take action steps to help, such as signing and sharing petitions, contacting your local representatives, boycotting unhealthful products, attending peaceful rallies, and so on.

Positive Thinking Alone Doesn't Cut It

In the past, Earth Angels avoided looking at these issues. They would try to use "positive thinking" as a way of dealing with the world. Well, positive thinking is important, as long as it includes taking positive *action steps,* too.

You can't clean your home with just positive thinking. You have to get out the broom and mop.

You can't feed your family with just positive thinking. You have to physically be involved in creating meals.

You can't keep your hair clean with just positive thinking. You have to take the action step of washing it with shampoo.

And it's the same with cleaning up and maintaining our world. You and I each have responsibilities to do our part. So to those of you who are taking action steps to help the planet, thank you a million times!

Standing up for what's right and being involved in issues that speak to your soul are part of the Earth Angel hero's journey. Sometimes, we are reluctant heroes who have a "calling" into service. Think of Joan of Arc . . . or in the realm of fiction, Frodo from *The Lord of the Rings,* Jake Sully in *Avatar,* and Dorothy in *The Wizard of Oz.*

Earth Angels and Narcissists

Earth Angels know what people want to hear and are intuitive. So we appeal to people's egos in an effort to please them, and their sense of entitlement grows. That makes us ripe targets for "narcissists," who are addicted to having their egos stroked by others.

"Pay no attention to that man behind the curtain!"

Those famous words from *The Wizard of Oz* perfectly apply to the eye-opening realizations we're having about how our world is really run. As the veil thins and the energy vibrations increase, we're clearly seeing the shockingly coldhearted truth behind some of our personal relationships and also the political machine, the oil and money barons, pharmaceuticals, pesticide companies that produce seeds for food, taxes, and the way in which people and animals are used as commodities without regard for truth or feelings.

Narcissists are those whose whole focus is their own needs and comfort. They don't have the ability to imagine how someone else feels, and they actually don't even care how others feel. The *Diagnostic and Statistical*

Manual of Mental Disorders (DSM-IV), used by therapists to diagnose mental illness and personality disorders, defines the Narcissistic Personality Disorder as someone having at least five of the following characteristics:

1. A grandiose sense of self-importance (e.g., the individual exaggerates achievements and talents and expects to be recognized as superior without commensurate achievements)

2. A preoccupation with fantasies of unlimited success, power, brilliance, beauty, or ideal love

3. A belief that he or she is special and unique and can only be understood by, or should associate with, other special or high-status people (or institutions)

4. A need for excessive admiration

5. A sense of entitlement (i.e., unreasonable expectations of especially favorable treatment or automatic compliance with his or her expectations); interpersonally exploitative (i.e., takes advantage of others to achieve his or her own ends)

6. A lack of empathy (is unwilling to recognize or identify with the feelings and needs of others)

7. Envy of others or a belief that others are envious of him or her

8. A demonstration of arrogant and haughty behaviors or attitudes

A narcissist surrounds him- or herself with people who agree with him or her, and anyone who dares to raise questions will be removed. A narcissist is terribly insecure and jealous, and views people and animals as objects to stroke his or her ego.

A sociopath (or psychopath) also views people and animals as objects. Like a narcissist, a sociopath has no empathy. Both narcissists and sociopaths know that they're unlike other people because they lack remorse or a conscience. But they hide this fact from others and pretend to feel guilty or sad as a manipulative tool. Their biggest manipulation, though, is that they twist other people—who *do* have a conscience—into feeling afraid or guilty so that they'll do what they want.

Sociopaths are often thought of as violent people, and that can be true. But there are nonviolent sociopaths who use other people to carry out their violent deeds. Unlike narcissists, who need other people to assure them of their superiority, sociopaths believe they *are* superior. They believe that people who have a conscience are weak and inferior. People and animals are pawns to entertain them and help them gain more money and power.

Both the narcissist and the sociopath need to dominate and control others. They'll both exploit you without any sense of guilt.

As we learn the truth about how the world operates, we see how sociopaths and narcissists have climbed to the top of the political scene. Since 96 percent of the population is estimated to have a normal conscience, we have been gullible in assuming that our leaders also had one. We've also submitted to their will, just like the behavioral studies predict.

Now that the veneer has been stripped away, what do we do?

1. We have spiritual power. Others can't contain, control, or tax your ability to use your mind to manifest,

pray, and think. This is why your angels are urging you to detox, as a sober mind is much more focused and powerful than an intoxicated or hungover mind. And this is why you're being urged to make the commitment to detoxify yourself.

You're much more powerful than you know, and you're in the good company of other lightworkers who care deeply about this planet. It will take some dedication, hard work, and self-analyzing to detox, but together we can do it!

2. Walk your talk. The fastest route to self-confidence is to act in accordance with your highest ideals. This doesn't mean you have to be perfect. In fact, perfectionism can make you feel bad about yourself. Instead, this means that you stop doing things you feel guilty about. It means regularly having honest conversations with yourself and adjusting your behavior accordingly. Ask your higher self: *What changes would you like to see me make, to be fully upon my highest path?*

3. Be familiar with the traits and tactics of narcissists and sociopaths. Knowledge and foresight are our best insurance when it comes to predicting their future behaviors and being prepared. Don't succumb to their fear- and guilt-inducing tactics. It's all smoke-and-mirrors games to them, and they're laughing at you the whole time that you're playing into their hands by reacting to fear and guilt.

4. Surround yourself with openhearted people. Now that you know how to spot a narcissist or sociopath, avoid them at all costs. They play cold and calculating games, and the only way to win is to drop out of the game.

Here's a wonderful prayer for dealing with narcissists, and for being an assertive Earth Angel activist:

"Dear God,
Thank You for guiding me to be a strong,
confident, and openhearted person.
Thank You for helping me find healthy
ways to deal with my emotions.
Thank You for guiding me to honor my body.
Thank You for sending me openhearted,
trustworthy, and nice friends.
Thank You for opening my eyes to the truth.
And thank You for watching over and protecting us all.
Amen."

AFTERWORD

The day that you no longer need others' approval is the day you have true freedom. Be real with people, and they'll respect you more . . . and most important, you'll respect *yourself* more.

You can find blessings and healing within every situation, including very sad and upsetting ones. And by doing so, you bring more healed and positive energy into this world.

You can shine your light more brightly by facing the feelings you're experiencing. Don't stuff them back down. Feelings are energy, and they need to flow and move.

You can only heal your old grief and anger by allowing these energies an opportunity for expression.

So express your feelings, please. Some examples of modes of expression are:

- Praying
- Creative and artistic projects
- Gardening or nature walks
- Journaling or blogging
- Talking to a trusted friend (living or deceased)
- Connecting with nature
- Engaging in your favorite activities
- Playing music
- Spending time with loved ones

One of my birthday traditions is to go to the gym and enjoy a nice leisurely workout. I began this tradition when I was 25 years old. Since then, I've worked out nearly every day as a gift that I give to myself.

On that day when I turned 25, I bought a membership at a local fitness center. I did this because I had meditated upon my life and asked for guidance on how to feel happier about myself. The inner answers I received were to exercise daily and also to "go for" my big desire to be a published author.

I realized that the only way to manifest my desires for greater fitness and to be published was for me to take action steps. My body would only get fit if I exercised it, ate healthfully, and stayed away from processed foods and harmful chemicals. And similarly, I'd only get published if I took the time to write daily and then submit my writing to a publisher.

Well, I did both! And because I put in the daily work of exercising and writing, my two visions of fitness and publication came true.

It wasn't because I was "lucky." Luck had nothing to do with it.

My dreams came true because I was willing to put in the time and the effort. I was a busy mom of two little boys, and I was going to college part-time *and* working full-time. So I had the perfect excuse to say that I didn't have the time, energy, or money to join a gym or write my book.

But excuses don't get you anywhere in life. Excuses are saying that you're a victim to outside circumstances, and that's never true.

Your ego's voice isn't your own. It's the voice of fear, and you don't have to listen to it or follow its dictates. Your ego always speaks about what you can't do. It starts sentences with *But . . .* such as "But I don't have enough time," or "But I need more money first," or "But what would people think?" The ego is a big "but"!

Don't allow your ego to talk you out of the joy that awaits you. The journey of pursuing your dreams is joyful. It's also ambiguous, uncertain, and unscripted. That's the artistic path of the soul.

So instead of listening to my ego's arguments, I chose a gym that had a fun day-care center for my sons, Charles and Grant, to stay in while I worked out. I knew it was good role-modeling for them to see their mother exercising regularly, just as I'd watched *my* mother do. I wanted my sons to learn healthful ways to deal with stress, through exercise, prayer, and meditation. And they did!

I also wanted to show my children that the universe would give us any gifts that we were willing to work toward.

And I wrote my books after my sons went to sleep at night. I created a calendar with self-imposed deadlines, which kept me motivated to finish each chapter.

And then I prayed and summoned the courage to submit those chapters to publishers.

Every dream you have works the same way. It's not enough to wish for something. It's not enough to pray for or visualize something.

God truly does help those who help themselves.

Instead of arguing why you *can't* do something, please try this lesson that I've learned and shared with you in this book:

Every day, take one action step related to your dreams. It doesn't matter what the action step is. What matters is that you expend daily effort in your desired direction.

Be your own authority figure and give yourself permission to make the changes you desire. You can make it happen with your clear decision, positive intentions, and willingness to do the necessary work and action steps.

This is a time of huge positive change and energy reassignments in the areas of home, relationships, and career. It's a perfect time to go for your dreams, even if you don't feel ready or clear about your entire action plan.

One step at a time, all dreams come true in ways that exceed your expectations . . . but you've got to make the first step!

No more self-doubts!

Whatever you set your mind to and are willing to work toward will happen . . . often in ways that are beyond your imagination.

Take risks and enjoy the journey. Stop playing life safe! And never underestimate the power of a determined Earth Angel (that means *you*).

God created everyone equally powerful.

Power doesn't come from money, education, or career titles.

Power comes from God. And you have already got this power right now.

Unleash your inner power for healing; creativity; and making positive changes for yourself, your loved ones, and this world.

All it takes is for you to believe in God's power, streaming through you.

Believe, and direct your inner power to bring healing light to the world.

Decide where to send your inner healing power, and then send it *now!*

With love,
Doreen

ABOUT THE AUTHOR

Doreen Virtue holds B.A., M.A., and Ph.D. degrees in counseling psychology. She's the author of over 50 books and oracle card decks dealing with spiritual topics. Best known for her work with the angels, Doreen is frequently called "The Angel Lady."

A lifelong activist, Doreen is involved in charities and movements that support a healthy environment, fair treatment of animals, clean air and water, and organic non-GMO food for all.

Doreen has appeared on *Oprah,* CNN, *The View,* and other television and radio programs, and writes weekly columns for *Woman's World* magazine. Her products are available in most languages worldwide, on Kindle and other eBook platforms, and as iTunes apps. For more information on Doreen and the workshops she presents, please visit: www.AngelTherapy.com.

You can listen to Doreen's live weekly radio show, and call her for a reading, by visiting HayHouseRadio.com®.

ANGEL THERAPY®

Hay House Titles of Related Interest

YOU CAN HEAL YOUR LIFE, the movie,
starring Louise L. Hay & Friends
(available as a 1-DVD program and an expanded 2-DVD set)
Watch the trailer at: www.LouiseHayMovie.com

THE SHIFT, the movie,
starring Dr. Wayne W. Dyer
(available as a 1-DVD program and an expanded 2-DVD set)
Watch the trailer at: www.DyerMovie.com

CALM: A Proven Four-Step Process for Women Who Worry,
by Denise Marek

*FROM MY HANDS AND HEART: Achieving Health and Balance
with Craniosacral Therapy,* by Kate Mackinnon

THE HOPE: A Guide to Sacred Activism, by Andrew Harvey

THE MAGIC PATH OF INTUITION, by Florence Scovel Shinn

THE POWER IS WITHIN YOU, by Louise L. Hay

TRUST YOUR VIBES: Secret Tools for Six-Sensory Living,
by Sonia Choquette

*THE TURNING POINT: Creating Resilience in a
Time of Extremes,* by Gregg Braden

All of the above are available at your local bookstore,
or may be ordered by contacting Hay House (see next page).

We hope you enjoyed this Hay House book. If you'd like to receive our online catalog featuring additional information on Hay House books and products, or if you'd like to find out more about the Hay Foundation, please contact:

Hay House, Inc., P.O. Box 5100, Carlsbad, CA 92018-5100
(760) 431-7695 or (800) 654-5126
(760) 431-6948 (fax) or (800) 650-5115 (fax)
www.hayhouse.com® • www.hayfoundation.org

Published and distributed in Australia by:
Hay House Australia Pty. Ltd., 18/36 Ralph St., Alexandria NSW 2015
Phone: 612-9669-4299 • *Fax:* 612-9669-4144 • www.hayhouse.com.au

Published and distributed in the United Kingdom by:
Hay House UK, Ltd., Astley House, 33 Notting Hill Gate,
London W11 3JQ • *Phone:* 44-20-3675-2450
Fax: 44-20-3675-2451 • www.hayhouse.co.uk

Published and distributed in the Republic of South Africa by:
Hay House SA (Pty), Ltd., P.O. Box 990, Witkoppen 2068
Phone/Fax: 27-11-467-8904 • www.hayhouse.co.za

Published in India by: Hay House Publishers India, Muskaan
Complex, Plot No. 3, B-2, Vasant Kunj, New Delhi 110 070 • *Phone:*
91-11-4176-1620 • *Fax:* 91-11-4176-1630 • www.hayhouse.co.in

Distributed in Canada by:
Raincoast, 9050 Shaughnessy St., Vancouver, B.C. V6P 6E5
Phone: (604) 323-7100 • *Fax:* (604) 323-2600 • www.raincoast.com

Take Your Soul on a Vacation

Visit www.HealYourLife.com® to regroup, recharge,
and reconnect with your own magnificence.
Featuring blogs, mind-body-spirit news, and
life-changing wisdom from Louise Hay and friends.

Visit www.HealYourLife.com today!